REAL ESTATE
CAREER STARTER

REAL ESTATE CAREER STARTER

by Mary Masi

LEARNINGEXPRESS

LearningExpress ◆ New York

Library of Congress Cataloging-in-Publication Data

Masi, Mary.
    Real estate career starter / by Mary Masi.
       p. cm. —(Career starters)
    ISBN 1–57685–142–7
    1. Real estate business—Vocational guidance. I. Title.
  II. Series.   98–24095
  HD1375.M357   1998   CIP
  333.33'023'73—dc21

Printed in the United States of America
9 8 7 6 5 4 3 2 1
First Edition

Regarding the Information in this Book
Every effort has been made to ensure accuracy of directory information up until press time. However, phone numbers and/or addresses are subject to change. Please contact the respective organizations for the most recent information.

For Further Information
For information on LearningExpress, other LearningExpress products, or bulk sales, please call or write to us at:
    LearningExpress™
    900 Broadway
    Suite 604
    New York, NY 10003
    212-995-2566

LearningExpress is an affiliated company of Random House, Inc.

ISBN 1–57685–142–7

7 85555 85142 9

CONTENTS

ABOUT THE AUTHOR | Mary Masi, M. A., is the founder of InfoSurge, a company specializing in writing, research, and editorial consulting. Previously, she worked in the editorial division of John Wiley & Sons, Inc., and before that, as a college English instructor.

INTRODUCTION

WHY ENTER THE REAL ESTATE FIELD?

Do you want to have the opportunity to earn a good living, meet lots of interesting people, and have flexible work hours? If so, a career in real estate may be for you. Real estate careers can be both personally and financially rewarding. Whether you are choosing your first career, or you are considering a career change, this book is for you. The book covers all the information you need to know to break into this exciting and diverse field, plus it gives you the inside scoop from successful real estate professionals. Their advice is invaluable to newcomers to the field.

While the majority of real estate professionals are residential sales agents or brokers, there are also many related real estate jobs in other areas. You might choose to specialize in commercial, industrial, or farm real estate sales, or you might enjoy property management or real estate appraisal. The possibilities seem endless when you start looking for career opportunities in the real estate field.

This fascinating and rewarding field is expected to grow through the year 2006. A wealth of openings for real estate agents and brokers will occur primarily due to replacement needs resulting from people transferring into other occupations or leaving the work force. Other real estate positions, such as property managers, may become available due to projected economic growth in the wholesale and retail trade, finance, insurance, and real estate fields. The changing demographic makeup of America will also create additional jobs for real estate property managers as the number of retirement communities and assisted living arrangements increase.

In chapter one, you'll get an inside look at what the best opportunities are in real estate today—from agent to broker to appraiser and more. This chapter contains useful information such as specific job descriptions, typical income levels, typical minimum requirements, trends in educational background, and fast-growing geographic locations for the hottest jobs in real estate. You'll find helpful advice from real estate professionals from across the country who give you the inside scoop on how to break into and succeed in this exciting field. Use the checklist at the end of the chapter to verify that real estate is indeed the career for you.

In chapter two, you'll see how to evaluate and select real estate training programs near you. You'll find sample courses that are taught in actual real estate training programs from different colleges and universities across the country. These course descriptions show you how long you need to go to school for each program, and they can help you decide which training program is right for you.

Chapter three contains a directory of real estate training programs that gives you a representative listing of schools across the country in order by city and state. So if you're considering moving to a new city, you can check that city's programs too. All training programs provide name, address, and phone number so you can contact each school directly to get more information and application forms.

After you've selected a training program that's right for you, you'll find out how you can use financial aid to help you pay for it in chapter four. It clearly explains the financial aid process step-by-step, so you can be prepared and receive your aid as soon as possible. Several helpful checklists and tables are included for your use. You'll also find out about tuition reimbursement programs that pay for your schooling.

Chapter five shows you how to land your first job. You'll find out how to use job directories and the Internet in your job search and how to evaluate different real estate companies. You'll find helpful advice on how to write your resume and ace your job interviews. Sample resumes and cover letters are included to guide you through the process.

Once you've completed your training program and landed your first job, chapter six shows you how to succeed on that job. You'll find out what qualities are rewarded, how to achieve professional success, and what specific advancement opportunities are available within the real estate field. You'll also find out what other career options and areas of specialization are available to you as you progress further in your career.

So read on to find out how you can land a job as a real estate professional and succeed in this exciting, demanding, and fulfilling career.

CHAPTER | 1

In this chapter, you'll find out what are the hottest job opportunities in real estate today, and how to launch a lucrative career in each of them. Plus, you'll get informative job descriptions and typical income levels for the hottest positions: agent, broker, appraiser, and property manager. Find out if a career in real estate is right for you by taking the quiz at the end of this chapter.

THE HOTTEST JOBS AND HOW TO GET THEM

The opportunities available in the real estate field today are many and varied. Few other careers offer the excitement, challenges, and income potential that this promising field does. Once you begin a career in real estate, you'll be a part of one of the largest industries in America today. Thousands of jobs will become available each year, and jobs in real estate sales will be especially plentiful, according to the Bureau of Labor Statistics.

Many jobs in the real estate field can be yours with a minimum of training, so you can get started on your path to success right away. Yes, believe it or not, you could be up and running in your new career within a few weeks or months. That's one of the advantages of entering the real estate field, and that reason—along with the high income potential— draws many people, both graduates who want to begin a new career fresh out of school and career-changers. On the other hand, many people today are pursuing college degrees in real estate and are entering the field with a solid educational background. The possibilities are endless in this diverse and gratifying field.

Numerous demands are placed on real estate professionals, and they often must wear many hats in the course of their workdays. These demands might include working odd hours, or answering a frantic phone call late at night about a seller agonizing over a buyer's offer. Or an appraiser may be faced with an antagonistic seller who thinks his business property should be valued several thousand dollars more than the figures allow. Perhaps a property manager is faced with a crisis just when she's trying to leave on a short weekend getaway. Indeed, the demands are many and varied in the real estate professional's life; however, along with them come many benefits.

WHY ENTER THE REAL ESTATE FIELD?

Many people are attracted to the real estate field, but not all for the same reasons. Most real estate professionals will tell you that they enjoy a variety of benefits working in the real estate field. Of course, an obvious benefit of real estate sales is the chance to make high commissions and earn a good living. But many sales agents also say they really enjoy the chance to meet new people and the variety of their workdays. Others value the benefit of getting the first crack at buying the best listings of homes for sale. Indeed, a large number of sales agents and brokers own real estate property for investment purposes, and they know enough about the business to make informed decisions on what property to buy and where.

Many of the people who are drawn into real estate don't like to get into dull routines, so the new people, new properties, and new situations they find every day is satisfying to them. Property managers often enjoy the mix of working with people and with numbers in their jobs. Appraisers often enjoy the variety of work settings they find themselves in. They are frequently out in the field, conducting research and performing appraisals of properties. Other real estate professionals who become well known in their community enjoy being recognized and respected at community gatherings and social events. There are many benefits to having a career in real estate—read on to find out more about the ones that appeal to you the most.

Flexible Work Schedule for Sales Agents

One of the reasons many people decide to get into real estate sales is because they do not want to sit behind a desk in an office job and work 9-to-5 for five days a week. The variety of the real estate professional's work schedule appeals to people who want flexibility and variety in their work tasks. Real estate sales offer individuals the opportunity to work part time if that is what fits their lifestyle best. Although the trend is for real estate sales agents to work full time, there are still many part-time workers in the field. If you need to take off several hours in the afternoon to go to a personal appointment or to attend a child's soccer game, you normally would have that flexibility. Of course, it may mean that you go out later that evening to show several homes to interested buyers. But for many salespeople, the flexibility of coming and going as they please is a big plus.

Autonomy for Brokers

Brokers who own their own real estate company enjoy a great level of autonomy. Their status as owners often brings them a high level of job satisfaction. While the pressures are high when you are the boss, so are the benefits of not having to answer to anyone else. For those brokers who are experienced and successful, their level of autonomy gives them great pleasure. (Of course, if you are floundering and profits are falling, you might prefer to pin it all on someone else instead of yourself.) A broker in St. Paul, Minnesota sums it up this way:

> I always wanted to work for myself, and I really hated having to punch a clock at my old job in my previous career as a car service manager. It was my incessant drive for autonomy that helped me make it through the lean years when I was struggling to get listings and sell homes when I first came into real estate. Well, after 11 years as a salesman and 3 as a broker, I feel that I have finally achieved my dream. I am now my own boss, and I love it. I answer to no one. This career has been a godsend for me.

Hard Work is Rewarded for Sales Agents

As a real estate sales agent, you probably won't see your coworkers being promoted to higher paying positions just because they are friends with the boss, even if they aren't selling any homes. Indeed, in the real estate business, the people who are rewarded are the ones who bring in the most and biggest commissions. Therefore, your rewards are in direct relation to the hard work you put in. As you gain experience, contacts, and referrals, you'll find that you have more bargaining power with your broker and may be able to negotiate a more favorable commission split. Sure, you can't get away completely from office politics, but if you're bringing in the big money, you can bet that you'll be treated well by your broker.

Job Satisfaction for Property Managers

Many on-site property managers enjoy helping the tenants in the buildings they manage. They gain great job satisfaction from helping someone to find the perfect apartment to rent or from giving someone a helping hand when disaster strikes in their unit. These managers spend a great deal of time ensuring the tenants in their buildings are safe, secure, and satisfied. They routinely handle emergencies with water, electricity, plumbing, gas, and other possible hazards.

Property managers who are not on-site also reap a good deal of job satisfaction. They enjoy knowing that they are successfully managing properties for the owners of those properties. Many times the owners do not even live in the same state as their property, so the owners are trusting the property managers with their oftentimes significant investment. When a property manager sees a way to cuts costs, improve services to the tenants, or lower the need for routine maintenance, he knows that he is doing an invaluable service for that property owner.

Appraisers Get Paid for Their Opinion

Many appraisers enjoy the fact that they are getting paid to offer their professional, sound opinion on the value of a property. That has to make you feel good! In what other career do you get paid to offer your opinion? Of course real estate appraisers must apply complex formulas and conduct rigorous research before they form a reasonable opinion about a property's value. A real estate appraiser in Las Vegas, Nevada shares her experience:

> The fact that I was being entrusted to come up with a value for a home made me feel great when I first got into this business. It was a little nerve-racking at first, but I learned a lot from my mentor. She

had been in the business for several years and was a veteran. I followed her around and studied every move she made until I felt comfortable with the whole process. It's a great thing to be able to provide this service because not that many people know how to do it.

Ease of Entrance from Another Career for Sales Agents/Brokers

Historically, real estate was a career that people came to later in life. Many sales agents made a transition into real estate from another career, such as office manager, sales representative, teacher, or homemaker. Nowadays, more and more people are majoring in real estate in college and are making real estate their first career. However, there are still many career-changers who enter the real estate field with a variety of other backgrounds. One of the reasons so many career-changers choose real estate is the ease of entrance requirements.

Most states require applicants to take a limited number of hours of real estate courses and pass a written exam before they can get their license to practice real estate sales. These requirements can often be met within a few months if you study on a regular basis and dutifully apply yourself to learning the material. Also, if you are entering real estate from a career in which you had considerable public contact, you may already have a wealth of possible contacts for getting listings and for selling properties. Don't underestimate the value of your current networking contacts for a new career in real estate.

Chance to Become Self-Employed

Many real estate professionals are self-employed, so they enjoy more freedom than employees who have a boss that they must answer to. Most sales agents work as independent contractors for their sponsoring broker. For those sales agents who apply themselves and pass the required courses and exam for becoming a broker, the possibilities just keep expanding. In many states, you can work for yourself as a broker in a one-person operation. This would mean keeping 100% of your commissions! You can even branch out after a few years and open your own office or buy into a real estate franchise opportunity and hire other sales agents to work for you, so you can get a percentage of the commissions they earn as well.

In addition to sales agents and brokers, a significant number of real estate appraisers and property managers also work for themselves. In fact, 4 out of 10 property managers were self-employed in 1996, according to the Bureau of Labor Statistics. Therefore, many entrepreneurial types are interested in becoming real estate professionals.

DO YOU HAVE WHAT IT TAKES?

Perhaps you are interested in getting into the real estate field, but you aren't sure what personality traits or personal abilities are needed for this exciting but challenging industry. Well, wonder no more! Here's the inside scoop from sales agents, brokers, appraisers, and property managers on what it takes to make it in real estate today.

Motivation

A certain amount of motivation is needed for performing almost any job. However, in real estate, it's of the utmost importance. It is especially important to be a self-starter in real estate sales because your motivation level can make or break your career. You probably won't have a boss standing over your shoulder telling you to make those extra cold calls or to spend that extra time organizing and expanding your contact list. It's up to you! If you have seen a pattern of motivation and diligence in your past, that's a good sign for a successful career in sales. On the other hand, if you need to have someone constantly reminding you to do something or if you feel that procrastination is your middle name, you may need to invest some time and money into motivation seminars if you really want to get into real estate sales.

Appraisers also mention motivation as a key to their success, especially the self-employed ones. It takes motivation to drum up new sales, attend conferences to get leads, and keep up with continuing education. Any type of work that you do as a self-employed person generally takes more self-motivation than when you have an employer telling you what to do. So take a few minutes to reflect on your level of self-motivation, and on your potential for increasing your motivation levels in the future.

Persistence

Being persistent can help you gain success in reaching any goal. In real estate, it's especially important to persist when times get tough. You'll encounter many deals in which conflicts arise or roadblocks pop up from out of nowhere. Perhaps it's the overbearing father-in-law who insists a particular house is not right for the young couple who adore it *after* they sign the contract. Or maybe a broker/owner is having trouble making ends meet during the first year of the new business. It is during these key times that persistence becomes especially important.

For a self-employed appraiser who is building up a client list, persistence can mean the difference between a thriving business in a couple of years, or a dead end. It takes time and effort to achieve success in this challenging field; many real estate professionals will tell you that their success really took off only after they'd been in the field for a few years. It was during the early years of laying the groundwork, putting in the time to get to know a neighborhood, making contacts, building a list of referrals, and advertising consistently that persistence was key.

Good Communication Skills

All real estate professionals need strong communication skills because real estate is a people business. Appraisers need to be able to communicate well both verbally and in writing because they spend hours conducting research, interviewing people, and writing reports. Those reports need to be clear and understandable to their target audience. Property managers also need to possess good communication skills because they are the conduits of information between tenants and owners. They must know how to interact with and please both sides. A property manager from Chicago, Illinois describes it this way:

> Oh, it's a challenge, all right. You have to constantly figure out ways to negotiate and mediate so each party feels that you are looking out for them. Of course, your main responsibility is to the owners since that is who pays you to manage their property. But it is an extension of that very responsibility that requires you to try and satisfy the tenants as well. If the tenants are happy, they pay their rent on time and the building stays occupied. If you get the tenants angry or can't calm them down or help them when they need you, they may leave and then you'll be stuck trying to explain that to the owners. So it's all a delicate balancing act that requires tact, good listening skills, and the ability to be objective and unemotional in the face of confrontation.

Mathematical Ability

Working with numbers is an important aspect of any real estate professional's job duties. While you don't need to be related to Einstein to be successful in real estate math, you do need to possess basic mathematical skills. For instance, the real estate licensing exam for sales agents and brokers normally devotes at least 15%–30% of the total number of questions to real estate math computations. However, don't let a lack of math skills scare you off from a career in real estate. You can probably master most if not all the math skills you need to pass the real estate licensing exam in a couple of weeks if you study and practice the skills every day. Several good books are available to help you learn and improve the math skills needed to pass the state licensing exam—see Appendix B for a list of relevant titles.

Obviously, real estate appraisers and property managers also use a significant amount of math in their daily job duties as well. Appraisers need math skills to estimate the current cost of reproducing a structure on the property they are appraising and figure out how much the value of an existing structure has depreciated over time when they use this appraisal method. Property managers often need to maintain detailed records of expenditures and income for each property they manage. Some may also need to project earnings and figure out expected income and expenses for a property to help the owners form strategic plans. Indeed, the amount of math, finance, and accounting skills needed varies considerably among property managers, depending on whether they are on-site managers working for a large firm, where another department may handle such things, or whether they own their own business and must perform all computations themselves.

Attention to Detail

While all real estate professionals need to be concerned with the details of their transactions, it is particularly important for appraisers to stay well on top of all the myriad of details in their work responsibilities. A real estate appraiser from Atlanta, Georgia describes the importance of details in this way:

> If I were to lose track of one little piece of information during the appraisal process, it could mean an alteration of the final estimate of value on the property. It is amazing how important each little detail is in this profession. It could be one clause in a zoning ordinance, or one mistake in a measurement taken, or missing something on a public record that could skew the end result. That's why I am painstakingly careful and retrace all my steps for each project to make sure every detail is correct and accounted for. You must be able to focus on the details and follow-up on each one to be sure you get the best estimate possible for each property you appraise.

Honesty

Many real estate professionals list honesty as the number one personal attribute needed in the real estate field. Due to the large amounts of money involved in each real estate transaction (indeed, many deals consist of a person's lifetime savings), honesty is of the utmost importance. When the stakes are high and you don't want to lose a deal, will you be tempted to cloud the truth or not disclose all relevant information that you are legally required to? This is a key issue that many real estate agents and brokers face on a regular basis. An experienced and successful real estate agent in St. Paul, Minnesota says:

> If you don't have a high degree of personal integrity and dedication to honesty, you can get into a lot of trouble in this field. Being dishonest can lead not only to the loss of repeat business from unsatisfied customers, but it can also lead to lawsuits and a revocation of your license. It really bugs me when I see other agents who are not completely honest with people. They give the rest of us a bad name. I just cannot emphasize it enough, honesty is number one.

Able to Handle Rejection and Disappointment

After spending many hours driving buyers around to look at home after home, a sales agent may find out that the buyers decided to purchase a home that was for sale by an owner. Or perhaps the buyer's cousin just obtained his real estate license, so they bought it through him instead. Agents must be able to handle this disappointment in a constructive way and realize that it's all a part of the job. A certain amount of uncertainty exists when working in this field and things won't always work out the way you'd like them to. Even if you invest considerable time and effort into making a sale, obstacles arise that may be out of your control. Therefore, you need to be able to move on and not let the disappointments get you down. If you are resilient, you will have a good shot at real estate success.

Management Skills

Brokers and office managers who own or manage a real estate office must have good management skills. It is not enough to know how to sell real estate if you want to run an office. You also need to possess good management skills. Luckily, there are many ways to obtain these skills. One of the most common ways is to take college courses in business management and finance from your local community college or university. Some of the franchise real estate businesses offer in-house management training to their office managers and brokers. Take advantage of any training opportunities that arise if you think you might want to get into management, either as an office manager or owner.

Trends in Educational Background

Real estate professionals in a variety of areas of specialization are increasingly obtaining higher levels of education than they have in the past. Indeed, many now have some college education, whether it be only a few courses, an associate degree, a bachelor's degree, or even in some cases, a master's or doctorate degree in real estate or a related area. While a college degree is not required to become a real estate sales agent or broker, you could benefit from taking at least some form of real estate courses. College courses in the following subject areas are especially useful to those planning to enter the real estate field:

- real estate
- finance
- economics
- marketing
- business administration
- psychology
- sociology
- architecture
- engineering

In addition to college courses, many private schools offer real estate training specifically tailored to help you pass the licensing exam in your state. See chapter two for more detailed information about the types of training programs and educational courses and degrees that are available, and how you can choose the one that's best for you.

Fast-Growing Geographic Locations

If you don't mind relocating in your quest for a successful career in real estate, there are areas of the country that are growing that are in need of real estate professionals. As you might guess, California is always the number one state for real estate deals. Other states that are growing include Florida, Arizona, Georgia, New Mexico, and Texas.

In addition to the southern and western states that are showing a great deal of growth, other opportunities exist in many states. Particularly, states that have a lot of farms and farmland near or within commuting distance to major cities offer opportunities for real estate professionals. These farms and farmland are being parceled off and sold to the highest bidder so builders can develop single family homes in deed-restricted communities on the land.

JOB OPPORTUNITIES IN THE REAL ESTATE FIELD

Many people are needed to list, sell, and appraise residential, commercial, industrial, and farmland properties. Additionally, other real estate professionals are needed to manage and lease commercial, industrial, and investment properties. The list goes on and on for the exciting job opportunities that are currently available in the real estate field.

Here are the hottest job opportunities for you to consider in this growing field. Look closely at the job description, typical minimum requirements needed, and typical income level for each job to help make your decision of where in real estate you want to build your career.

Residential Real Estate Sales Agent

Residential sales agents have what is probably the most widely known position in the real estate field. Their faces may be on billboards, in glossy magazines, and on magnets or other promotional giveaways because they are always looking for ways to gain more business. The sales agent's job revolves around contact with people.

Residential sales agents list homes for sale, and they sell homes that they or other agents have listed. While some homeowners attempt to sell their own home, many more homeowners decide to list their home for sale through a real estate salesperson. This is one of the major ways residential agents earn their living— through getting new people to list their homes for sale with them. Agents normally perform a market analysis on each home they list to determine a fair selling price. They do this by comparing the home to be sold with other similar homes in the neighborhood that have recently been sold.

Another way agents earn their living is through selling homes that are currently listed for sale either by them or by an agent who subscribes to the multiple listing service (MLS). The MLS is a complex computer network of homes for sale that have been listed by real estate sales agents or brokers. Agents meet with potential buyers to get a sense of the type of home they want and can afford. Many agents will "pre-qualify" their buyers by completing a form to see how much the buyers can afford to pay for a home based on income and debt figures. Agents then normally drive buyers around to look at relevant homes, or they show buyers video footage of homes. Sales agents submit offers from buyers to sellers and may also deal with counter offers.

Historically, sales agents worked on behalf of the seller, not the buyer, even though they spent a good deal of time driving buyers around to look at homes. However, today, many agents are now working as "buyer's agents" or performing what is called "dual agency," in which they represent both parties. It is the agent's responsibility to inform all parties to any real estate transaction what role he is playing. Many agents present their role in writing and have the buyer and seller sign it to clear up any possible confusion. Becoming a buyer's agent is an emerging trend in residential real estate, so you should watch out for anything that relates to the topic of "agency" when you take your pre-licensure course(s). See chapter two for more information about real estate courses and training programs.

Residential real estate sales agents are normally independent contractors, not employees, and they earn their living by getting commissions on the homes they list and sell. They normally do not earn salaries or get an hourly wage. While this method of payment may seem a bit scary at first glance, upon reflection, you'll see that there is almost limitless income potential. If you have the talent, drive, and ambition, you can list and sell homes until you become quite wealthy. It is this potential for significant earnings that draws many people into the residential real estate sales field.

Typical Minimum Requirements

All states require that real estate salespeople become licensed before they can sell or list real estate. While requirements vary depending on what state you want to get your license in, a few standard minimum rules apply: you must be over 18 years old and possess a high school diploma or its equivalent. In most states, you must be affiliated with a real estate broker before you can get your real estate agent's license. Brokers own or manage the real estate office from which you'll be working as an agent.

Since every state has its own specific licensing requirements, you'll need to contact your state real estate commission or licensing agency (see Appendix A for contact information) to find out what your state's requirements are. For instance, many states require you to complete a state-approved real estate course or training program before you can take the licensing exam. Even in states that do not require such formal training, many applicants pursue real estate courses anyway to be sure they know the material well enough to pass the licensing exam. See chapter two for more information about the real estate exam and other licensing and certification requirements.

Typical Income Level

Income levels vary greatly depending on the location and the size of the real estate company and more importantly, the experience and talent of individual sales agents. According to the Bureau of Labor Statistics, an average annual income level for full-time real estate agents, brokers, and appraisers was $31,500 in 1996. Several residential sales agents work part time, and some have other related businesses in addition to real estate sales. People who have been in the business for many years and get a lot of repeat business and referrals from satisfied customers may make significantly more money per year. In fact, some residential real estate agents list and sell million-dollar homes—just think of their commissions!

Commission rates on the sale of a home normally range from 5-10 %, with an average of 6%. Each commission earned by a sales agent is normally shared with the sales agent's broker, in a ratio that is mutually agreed upon when you join the company. The split is often 50:50. However, experienced sales agents may be able to negotiate a much better ratio, and may get as much as 70:30, 80:20 or more if they bring in the heaviest volume of sales on a consistent basis. If you list a home and another sales agent sells it, or vice versa, then the commission is first split 50:50 between your broker and the other agent's broker. Therefore, if you list and sell the same home, your commission will be much higher than if you perform only one of these functions for any particular home.

Residential Real Estate Broker

Real estate brokers own or manage the company that sales agents work for. They often were sales agents themselves, who decided to move ahead in their careers by either going into management in a large firm, starting a franchise, or branching out and starting their own business. Sponsoring brokers are normally legally responsible for the work of their sales agents. It varies widely how involved brokers are in the daily operations of the sales agents. Some brokers closely supervise all of their agents, or at least the new ones. Other brokers spend a lot of their time continuing to sell properties to bring in more commissions to the office and leave the sales agents to fend for themselves, more or less. You'll find out more about management styles of brokers and how they impact their sales agents in chapter five. Brokers often manage the advertising of the homes their sales agents list, oversee general administrative duties of running an office, and may help to train new salespeople. Some sales agents become brokers and continue to work under the auspices of another broker. These people are often called associate brokers.

Typical Minimum Requirements

While minimum requirements vary depending on what state you want to get a broker's license in, you normally must be at least 18 years of age and possess a high school diploma or its equivalent. In addition, brokers need to pass a written exam to become licensed, and in many states, they are required to attend from 50–90 hours or more of real estate broker training. Some states also require brokers to have from 1–3 years of experience as a real estate sales agent before they can apply to become a broker. However, in many cases a bachelor's degree in real estate may be substituted for the sales experience.

Typical Income Level

Brokers receive the real estate commission for each sale that their agents make, and they split that commission with the agent. The ratio is normally 50:50 for new salespeople. Many brokers will entice their best agents to stay with them by sharing more and more of the commission with them, sometimes going as high as 20:80 in favor of the salesperson. In certain offices, brokers let their sales agents keep 100% of their commissions—the brokers make their money by charging hefty desk fees, which may range from a few hundred dollars to well over a thousand dollars a month.

Brokers who own large real estate firms with many successful sales agents have the potential for earning a significant amount of money each year. However, brokers normally don't start out in such a good place. Many new brokers have to struggle to make ends meet and may have to log in several hours to keep the company afloat until it starts to earn significant commissions. The average annual income for full-time brokers, sales agents, and appraisers in 1996 was $31,500, according to the Bureau of Labor Statistics. Of course, many experienced brokers earn significantly more than that.

Commercial Real Estate Agents and Brokers

Commercial real estate agents and brokers do many of the same things residential agents and brokers do, but for different types of property. Instead of selling and listing homes, these agents and brokers are selling, listing, and leasing commercial properties. These properties may include shopping centers, apartment complexes, movie complexes, small businesses, large corporate offices, and other income producing properties.

As you might guess, there are not nearly as many agents and brokers specializing in commercial properties as there are in residential real estate. This point is easy to figure out. Take a look around your neighborhood at how many homes and condominiums there are compared to how many commercial buildings there are. However, what commercial real estate lacks in volume, it makes up for in excitement and rewards, due to the complex deals that need to be negotiated. But along with the excitement and rewards that would lure newcomers into this field comes the potential for starvation before earning commissions. Many commercial real estate deals take 9–10 months or more to close because so many people are involved in each transaction. So you need to either have excellent credentials (such as a master's degree or two in real estate and related areas) or a good network of contacts if you want to close one or more commercial deals within your first six to twelve months in the business.

Here are some common commercial real estate areas of specialization:

- office building sales
- office leasing
- retail sales
- retail leasing
- investment property sales
- apartment building sales
- hotel sales
- restaurant sales
- land sales
- manufactured home parks

Typical Minimum Requirements

The minimum requirements for becoming a commercial real estate agent or broker are exactly the same as for becoming a residential agent or broker. Therefore, technically speaking, any residential real estate sales agent or broker can sell, list, or lease commercial real estate. However, the reality is that most do not. It's a highly competitive field and many sales agents and some brokers are not interested in learning and dealing with all the intricacies of this specialized market.

Typical Income Level

Agents and brokers who specialize in commercial real estate usually do not make as many sales as residential agents and brokers, but the commissions on the few sales they do close are often quite substantial. However, many sales agents do not earn enough commissions to pay their living expenses for at least a year. Indeed, many agents don't realize a steady and significant income for 2–5 years after starting their specialization. But for those agents who pay the price and make it through the first few lean years, the financial rewards can be tremendous. Many successful commercial agents and brokers may earn from $100,000 to $1,000,000 in a good year.

Industrial Real Estate Agents and Brokers

Industrial real estate agents and brokers perform tasks similar to commercial agents and brokers. The difference is that they focus on selling or leasing property that is used for industry or manufacturing. So, the types of properties they deal with include warehouses, industrial plants, and factories. Industrial sales agents and brokers need to understand the local zoning laws that apply to each property under consideration. Perhaps some buyers will want to expand an existing factory to accommodate their operating volume, but if that is against the zoning requirements for that piece of property, the agent would need to inform the buyers.

Industrial sales agents also need to know extensive information about the surrounding community if the buyer plans to employ a large number of employees. How is the labor market in the area? Are there adequate resources for the employees who will live near the factory or plant? Are there appropriate forms of transportation, both to get employees and supplies to the job site and to ship out the goods once they are manufactured? You can see that a whole new set of skills and information is needed for specializing in industrial real estate. In addition to convincing buyers that a particular property is the perfect spot for them to relocate to, you'll need to help them finance the deal. If the financing doesn't go through, there is no deal, and you don't get your commission. So, just as in residential real estate where sales agents help the financing process along, you'll need to know how to help the financing process along in industrial real estate.

Typical Minimum Requirements

Theoretically, any residential real estate sales agent or broker can sell, list, or lease industrial real estate since the minimum requirements for becoming an industrial real estate agent or broker are exactly the same as for becoming a residential agent or broker. In reality, however, most do not. It's a highly competitive field and many residential sales agents do not want to deal with the complexities of industrial real estate.

Typical Income Level

Similar to commercial agents and brokers, industrial agents and brokers do not close as many sales as residential agents and brokers, but the sales they do close net them large commissions. However, since deals take so long to close in the industrial arena, sales agents and brokers often face a severe lack of earnings when first entering the field. Significant earnings can take anywhere from 1–5 years to achieve.

Farm and Farmland Agents and Brokers

If your background includes living on or near a farm, you'll have a headstart on specializing in farm and farmland sales. Knowing general background information about farms and farmland before you enter this area of specialization will be a big help. But don't despair, if you grew up in New York City and never even saw a cow or a goat before, you can learn the background information needed to succeed in farm sales. It just may take you a while longer to learn all the information that's needed. You'll need to know quite a bit about all of the following:

- crop values
- tax incentive programs for farmers
- value of farm equipment
- value of farm animals
- types of soil
- climate
- water rights
- drainage
- minerals
- land leases

So your first step is to gain the knowledge you need to converse with farmers and interested buyers by taking courses in farm and farmland sales. Check with your local real estate schools to see if they offer such courses. Another option is to take the course on land brokerage that is sponsored by the Farm and Land Institute (the Farm and Land Institute is a branch of the National Association of Realtors). See Appendix A for contact information.

Typical Minimum Requirements

The minimum requirements for listing and selling farm and farmland real estate are the same as for the residential real estate sales agent and broker. However, due to the specialized nature of the field, you'll obviously want to gain an understanding of farms and their value before branching out into this area. This is a small niche market, so many real estate agents and brokers are not involved in selling, listing, or leasing farms, or at least not exclusively. Many real estate agents will occasionally sell a farm or some farmland but not on a regular basis.

Typical Income Level

Again, since sales agents and brokers who sell farms and farmland often do so in conjunction with other real estate, such as residential or commercial, their earnings are usually mixed. It may take anywhere for a year or more to close on selling a farm, but if that commission is worth $20,000 to $25,000, it can be well worth it. It's difficult to gauge a typical income level for farm and farmland sales agents because so many of them do not sell and list farms exclusively. If you take the average income level for a residential real estate sales agent and then add in an occasional farm commission or two, you'll get the picture.

Real Estate Appraiser

Real estate appraisers estimate the market value of properties. They investigate the quality of construction, the overall condition of the property, and its functional design. They gather information on properties by taking measurements, interviewing persons familiar with the property's history, and searching public records of sales, leases, assessments, and other transactions. Appraisers may compare a property with other similar properties for which recent sale prices or rental data are available to help them arrive at an estimate of value. In other cases, appraisers estimate the costs of reproducing the structure on the property and add that to the value of the land, and then combine that information with how much the value of the existing structure has depreciated. For rental properties, an appraiser may estimate the current and future income generated by the rental of the property to determine its current value.

Appraisers, therefore, spend a lot of time outside of their offices conducting research to determine a property's value. They need to possess strong research, organization, and math skills and should also be detail oriented. They may also need to understand blueprints and survey drawings. Appraisers normally devote a portion of their monthly work schedule to keeping up with the latest government regulations and economic trends both nationally and in their local region.

Several changes occurred in the appraisal industry resulting from Title XI of the federal legislation entitled Financial Institutions Reform, Recovery, and

Enforcement Act of 1989 (FIRREA). This legislation requires appraisers to be state licensed or certified in order to conduct federally related real estate transactions and to follow the Uniform Standards of Professional Appraisal Practice (USPAP). These professional standards are constantly changing, so appraisers who work on federal projects continually seek information about the changes and regulations to remain up-to-date.

Many appraisers choose to specialize in one area, so they can increase their knowledge and expertise in that area and gain a reputation in one particular specialization, such as single-family homes, multiple-family homes, apartment complexes, condominiums, commercial property, public housing, or other niche market. The services of real estate appraisers may be required by any of the following:

- banks
- mortgage lenders
- investors
- home buyers
- home sellers
- insurance companies
- developers
- corporations
- tax assessor's office

Several job opportunities exist for real estate appraisers with government agencies, large real estate offices, banks, insurance companies, tax assessor firms, and appraiser consulting firms, in addition to becoming self-employed.

Typical Minimum Requirements

The trend is for prospective appraisers to graduate from college with a degree in business administration, real estate, finance, or related field and then start their career by becoming a trainee and working with an experienced appraiser for several months to a year or more. Historically, many appraisers without a college degree came into the field from another real estate specialty, such as sales or brokerage, and some appraisers still enter the field that way today.

The federal government has been instituting tighter restrictions and stricter certification requirements for appraisers who perform work for the federal government. Indeed, real estate appraisers must now be licensed or certified by their state to appraise certain types of federally related real estate transactions. Many appraisers are members of a professional appraisal society or association to help them stay current on all the latest requirements and to achieve specific appraisal designations or certifications.

Each state has its own licensing requirements for real estate appraisers. However, to get licensed, these general conditions normally apply: passing a standardized test, taking a certain number of approved appraisal courses and getting a certain amount of on-the-job experience.

Typical Income Level

In direct contrast to real estate sales agents and brokers, real estate appraisers do not receive commissions based on the value of the property they assess. In fact, it is against the law for appraisers to get this type of a commission—the appraisal needs to be accurate and honest, and what a temptation there would be to inflate the value if one's income was based on that value! Most appraisers are paid a flat fee for each project, and many appraisers are self-employed. Others may work for an appraisal consulting firm or other organization and receive a set salary or a commission based on the number of projects completed. The standard flat fee for appraising a home is approximately $200–$300. Of course, that fee may be higher or lower in certain parts of the country or for certain homes that require more complex appraisals.

Real Estate Property Managers

Real estate property managers manage property that is owned either by themselves or another owner. Their responsibilities range from living on-site and collecting rent in an apartment complex to managing several on-site managers from a remote location. Property managers may be responsible for maintaining commercial or residential real estate, or both, depending on the size and expertise of the property management firm. Some firms are one-person operations that consist of a self-employed property manager. Others may be large corporations that employ hundreds of property managers and administrative workers who handle the paperwork involved in property management.

The responsibilities of property managers vary depending on the type of property they are managing, the number of properties they are managing, and the relationship they have to the owner(s) of the property. Many property managers work on-site. That is, they live on the premises of the property they manage, such as apartment complexes, condominiums, and multi-family homes. They take care of collecting the rent and negotiating contracts for services such as security, cleaning crews, landscapers, trash collectors, and repair workers. Obviously, the complexity of this job ranges a great deal depending on the type and size of the property that is being managed. Many other property managers do not live on-site, but they manage a large number of the daily operations from an off-site location, perhaps for several different properties.

In addition to managing the daily operations of a property, many property managers need to be well versed in applicable laws, tax regulations, and other administrative knowledge. They need to be aware of local and national housing laws, such as the Americans With Disabilities Act and the Federal Fair Housing Amendment Act. Many property managers also complete detailed reports regarding the property's income and expenses for submission to the owner. They also often show rental properties and explain the lease terms and property regulations to prospective tenants.

Many property managers specialize in one or more of the following areas:

- single family homes
- two to six family homes (also known as duplexes, triplexes, six-plexes, etc.)
- apartment complexes
- condominiums
- homeowner associations
- asset management
- land development

Asset Managers

The property managers who specialize in asset management purchase, develop, and sell properties for individual and business investors. Historically, asset managers were referred to simply as property managers; however, an emerging trend is to make a distinction between the two groups and refer to these professionals as real estate asset managers instead. This trend is being encouraged by professional associations, such as the American Society of Asset Managers. Property managers who manage assets perform long-term strategic financial planning and have an overview of the financial aspects of each deal instead of focusing on the daily operations of the property. They need to be familiar with several real estate principles in order to make the best decision on whether to buy or sell a particular property. Some of these issues may include:

- property value
- tax rates

- population growth
- zoning regulations
- traffic patterns and volume
- mortgage terms
- creative financing

Land Development Managers

Another area of specialization for property managers is to work for land development companies. These property managers acquire land and plan the construction of commercial buildings on that land. This is a complex job that is similar to the position of land developer (discussed in chapter six). Land development managers interact with several different people to bring a construction project to fruition. They spend a great deal of time negotiating with professionals in various local, state, or federal government offices, public utilities, community organizations, finance companies, mortgage lenders, architectural and design firms, construction companies, lobbying groups, and other businesses.

Typical Minimum Requirements

The typical minimum requirements for becoming a property manager vary depending on the type of property management you want to do. Many managers enter the field by gaining work experience as an on-site manager at an apartment complex, condominium, or homeowner association or as an assistant manager in a large property management company. Many prospective property managers attend or graduate from college to land entry-level management jobs in the field, although a college degree is not required for all property management jobs. However, if you want to specialize in asset management or land development you'll probably need either significant experience in the field or a high level of training, such as a bachelor's degree in real estate, finance, or management. Indeed, many more large employers are now requiring entry-level property managers to hold a college degree in business administration, real estate, or a related field.

Typical Income Level

Income levels vary depending on the type, size, and location of properties that are managed, as well as the area of specialization that a property manager is in. The average annual earnings for all property managers as a whole was $28,500 in 1996, while the top ten percent of property managers earned more than $60,700, according to the Bureau of Labor Statistics. Approximately 4 out of 10 property managers are self-employed. Many managers receive a percentage of the rent that is generated from the properties they manage. Several on-site managers receive an apartment to live in rent-free as a part of their compensation. Property managers who specialize in land development property management often receive a small percentage of the profits from the properties they develop.

IS A CAREER IN REAL ESTATE RIGHT FOR YOU?

After reading the job descriptions listed above for the hottest positions in the real estate field, you are now ready to take the following test to see if you are really cut out for a real estate career. You must be interested in the real estate field, or you wouldn't be reading this book, but are you indeed a good match for real estate? Read on to find out!

Should You Enter the Real Estate Field?

Find out if you really are suited to becoming a real estate professional! Jot down your answers to the following questions and then take a look at what those answers mean by reading the paragraph after the test.

1. Do you have a genuine liking for people?
2. Do you appreciate having variety in your work day?
3. Are you good at math?
4. Are you a self-starter?
5. Do you have good listening skills?
6. Do you like to have a high degree of security in your life?
7. Do you prefer working alone more than with other people?
8. Do you have a hard time motivating yourself to do things?
9. Do you enjoy a daily routine that is the same every day?
10. Do you value a high level of privacy and quiet time when you are at work?
11. Do you enjoy negotiating?
12. Do you enjoy working in a variety of environments?
13. Are you tactful and attentive to other people's needs?
14. Do you present yourself in a professional manner?
15. Are you good at solving problems?
16. Do you feel that weekends should be spent with your friends or family?

17. Do you dread calling people you don't know?
18. Do you get especially nervous when meeting new people?
19. Do you have trouble displaying self-confidence?
20. Do you pay close attention to details?
21. Are you extremely organized?
22. Do other people consider you friendly?
23. Do you enjoy getting involved in community events?
24. Do you enjoy meeting and talking to a variety of people?
25. Are you honest and trustworthy?

If you answered *yes* to the majority of questions numbered 1–5, 11–15, and 21–25, and *no* to the majority of questions 6–10 and 16–20, then you'll probably want to go full steam ahead toward a real estate sales agent or broker career.

However, if you answered *yes* to the majority of questions numbered 6–10, and 16–20, and *no* to the majority of questions 1–5, 11–15, and 21–25, then you may want to consider one of the related jobs in real estate. Jobs that don't center quite so squarely on selling and that provide a steady income and a more routine workday would probably better suit you—such as a mortgage broker or title searcher.

THE INSIDE TRACK

Who:	James Paxton
What:	Broker/Owner of Century 21 Aspen
Where:	New Mexico
How long:	Nineteen years in the real estate field

Insider's Advice

Find out what you are best at and what you enjoy—is it selling or management? That is a key to planning your real estate career path. Some sales agents decide to become a broker and open their own company or join with one or more partners only to find that they aren't cut out for the management role that is needed to succeed as an owner/broker. They miss the selling aspect, so they go back to working for another broker and begin selling again full-time. You need to have experience or training in management to succeed as an owner of a real estate office; strong selling skills alone are not enough.

If you are considering investing the time and money needed to get a real estate salesperson's license, first do some research on what it is like to be a salesperson. Observe people who are currently working in residential real estate sales. Ask to spend some time with a sales agent, so you can see just what he encounters throughout his workday. You need to find out if you would be comfortable working in sales or not. It is better to find out if you like sales before you make a commitment to fulfilling all the real estate license requirements in your state. One question to ask yourself is "How do I feel about constantly meeting people I don't know?" Your answer to this question is important.

Insider's Take on the Future

There seem to be more people entering real estate sales now who had another career previously. For example, school teachers, police officers, or others who have retired from their first career are finding success as real estate sales agents. One of the advantages of a career in residential sales is that it doesn't require one particular personality type, education level, or background. More important that these things are a person's self-motivation and talent for selling.

I don't actively recruit new salespeople because of the high retention rate of current salespeople in my office. However, many other companies are constantly advertising for new sales agents. The volume of new agent recruiting depends on the particular company and its salesperson retention rate. If you have motivation and integrity and if you enjoy meeting new people and making sales, you can build a successful career in real estate sales.

CHAPTER | 2

This chapter explains the many types of training that are available for becoming a real estate professional. You'll see several real estate program descriptions from a variety of schools and find inside tips on how to evaluate training programs. Plus, you'll get up-to-date information on the latest licensing and certification requirements for sales-people, brokers, and appraisers.

ALL ABOUT TRAINING PROGRAMS

You can take several different routes to getting the real estate training you need. Below are descriptions of the major types of training programs that are available for all experience levels ranging from high school to bachelor's degrees.

HIGH SCHOOL PREPARATION

If you haven't yet completed high school, you can take courses that will help you to prepare for entering the real estate field. First of all, make sure that you have a handle on basic skills such as reading comprehension, writing, computer literacy, and basic mathematics. To increase your preparation, take as many of the following classes as possible:

- Business Math
- Social Studies
- History
- Foreign Language

- ◆ Communications
- ◆ English
- ◆ Office Skills

By building a strong educational foundation while still in high school, you'll increase your chances of succeeding in the next phase of your training, whether it's a certificate, an associate degree, or a bachelor's degree.

Preparing for the State Licensing Exam

If your state requires proof of completion of one or more real estate courses prior to taking a real estate licensing exam, then you'll need to investigate which schools offer these courses. Contact your state's real estate commission, licensing agency, or appraisal board (see Appendix A for contact information) to find out what educational requirements need to be met and to get a list of schools that provide the necessary training in your state.

You'll often have a variety of schools and programs to choose from. For example, Idaho has 15 certified schools that offer state-approved real estate courses to prepare applicants for the state licensing exam, including two correspondence course programs. Their list includes small proprietary schools (private schools) and major public universities.

There's quite a range among states of education requirements that are needed to get a real estate salesperson's license: Massachusetts only requires 30 hours of pre-licensing education, but Kentucky requires 96 hours. There are no federal rules about how much pre-licensing education is needed for salespeople, so each state is free to set its own guidelines.

Samples of Required Courses

While each state sets its own standards and requirements for which classes, if any, applicants must take before sitting for a real estate licensing exam, you're probably curious to know what some of these classes are like. Here's a sampling of real estate courses you might need to take. Of course, these are just samples—you should contact your real estate commission or appraisal board to find out their specific and up-to-date requirements.

Pre-license Salesperson Educational Requirements in Western State
Essentials of Real Estate (45 hours)

This fundamental course covers topics such as real estate license law, property rights, contracts, finance, legal language, and deeds.

Real Estate Practices (45 hours)

Students take this course after completing the Essentials of Real Estate to learn more detailed real estate information, such as principles of listing, buying, closing, and selling homes.

Pre-license Salesperson Educational Requirement in Midwestern State
Principles and Practices of Real Estate (60 hours)

Subjects that need to be covered include property management/leasing, Iowa License Law, property ownership, encumbrances, legal descriptions, titles, closings, contracts, agency, antitrust, valuation, finance, math, and fair housing.

*Note: home study courses do not fulfill the pre-license educational requirement.

Pre-license Salesperson Educational Requirements in Southern State

Principles of Real Estate (30 hours)

Law of Agency (30 hours)

Law of Contracts (30 hours)

Additional core or related courses (90 hours)

Total required hours of real estate courses is 180.

Other Core Real Estate Courses

Topics include contract forms, finance, marketing, math, property management, investments, real estate law, and residential inspection.

Related Real Estate Courses

Topics may include titles, closings, taxation, ethics, syndication, farm and ranch properties, construction, real estate trends, or other approved related course.

Pre-license Broker Educational Requirements in Southeastern State

Completion of Salesperson pre-license educational requirements (90 hours)

Broker Real Estate Approved Courses (150 hours):

- Louisiana Real Estate License Law
- Commission Rules/Regulations
- Civil Law Pertaining to Real Estate
- Related Real Estate Subjects

Pre-license Appraiser Educational Requirements in Southern State

Fundamental Real Estate Appraisal Courses (30 hours)

Uniform Standards of Professional Appraisal Practice (USPAP) Courses (15 hours)

Courses must cover these subjects:

Influences on Real Estate Value, Legal Considerations in Appraisal, Types of Value

Economic Principles, Real Estate Markets and Analysis, Valuation Process, Property Descriptions, Highest and Best Use Analysis, Appraisal Statistical Concepts, Site Value

Sales Comparison Approach, Cost Approach, Income Approach, Appraisal Standards and Ethics

Additional courses related to real estate appraisal (15 hours)
Courses may include the following:

Real Estate Appraisal, Real Estate Principles, Real Estate Law, Real Estate Finance, Real Estate Mathematics, Real Estate Management, Property Management, Real Estate Investments

Total of 90 classroom hours is required.

Certificate Programs

Certificate programs range from a few weeks in a private real estate school to several months of college courses at a community college. You may decide to explore different areas of real estate or delve further into topics that interest you by completing one or more certificate programs. Many community colleges and business schools offer certificate programs in real estate.

You'll want to investigate several schools to find the one that is best for you. The directory of schools that offer real estate training programs listed in chapter three is a great place for you to start your training program search. Of course, not all of the real estate programs in the country could be provided within the allotted space, but the list can give you a good start by showing you a representative listing of schools in each state.

Additionally, several professional associations also offer certificates or professional designations for a particular area of specialization. However, many of these courses are geared toward people who have already joined a profession and have considerable experience in the field. Therefore, these types of certificates and professional designations are discussed in more detail in chapter six, which focuses on how to succeed in the real estate field.

Read all certificate materials carefully before you apply to any program of study. You should also speak to an instructor or guidance counselor at the schools you are considering to find out if the real estate certificate they offer is a good match for you. There may be more than one certificate offered by a school that falls under the general heading of *Real Estate*, so you need to examine each certificate program carefully before enrolling. Most certificate programs require that applicants have a high school diploma or its equivalent before beginning the certificate program.

An example of a typical real estate certificate training program is listed below to give you an idea of what you can expect to find in a similar training program near you. This training program is offered at a community college in Colorado. State residents pay $54 per credit. Non-residents of Colorado pay $252 per credit.

Sample Certificate Program #1	
Course Name	Number of Credit Hours
Real Estate Practice and Law	4
Colorado Contracts and Regulations	4
Trust Accounts and Record Keeping	1
Current Legal Issues	1
Real Estate Closings	3
Practical Applications	3
Total Credits Required for Certificate	**16**

It is typical for programs to require regular attendance and an academic average of a "C" or higher (2.0 GPA) to be eligible to receive a certificate upon completion of the course.

Certificate degree programs vary in content and length depending on what school and state you are in. For instance, take a look at the certificate program in real estate that is shown below. This one is offered at a community college in California and is much longer than the one listed above that is in Colorado. This certificate program requires a total of 30 units (or credit hours). The tuition for California residents is free; residents pay approximately $330 in fees per year. The tuition for non-residents of California is approximately $2,850 annually.

Sample Certificate Program #2	
Course Name	Number of Credit Hours
Real Estate Principles	3
Real Estate Finance	3
Real Estate Economics	3
Real Estate Appraisal	3
Advanced Real Estate Appraisal	3
Real Estate Finance	3
Real Estate Investments	3
Real Property Management	3
Agency, Corporations, and Partnerships	3
Business Mathematics	3
Total Credits Required for Certificate	**30**

Associate Degrees

An associate degree program's length of study for full-time students is two academic or two calendar years. Entrance requirements include a high school diploma or a GED, and some programs may require that applicants take high school college preparatory courses in order to gain admission. Many associate degree programs require students to take entrance and placement exams.

There are different associate degrees that you can earn—the most common ones are the associate of arts, associate of science, and the associate of applied science. Typically, the associate of arts degree is for students who plan to transfer to a four-year college or university and want an education with a liberal arts emphasis to prepare them for this transfer. Courses are normally required in the humanities, sciences, and business. Several areas of emphasis may be offered, including art, economics, English, foreign language, history, political science, psychology, and so on. The associate of science degree is also for students who want to transfer to a four-year college or university, but who wish to focus on science. Courses include biology, biotechnology, chemistry, computer science, preparatory engineering, geology, mathematics, physics, and so on.

The associate of applied science is geared for students who want to prepare for or upgrade their skills for employment in a career-oriented program of study. While the degree is not intended for students who plan to transfer to a four-year college or university, some individual courses may be transferable. Many areas of emphasis are offered in the associate of applied science degree, such as real estate, marketing, human resources management, legal secretary, accounting, and financial services management.

Read all college materials carefully before you apply to an associate degree program. You should also speak to an instructor or guidance counselor at the school you are considering to find out if the real estate associate degree it offers is a good match for you. There may be several different courses offered by one school that fall under the general heading of *Real Estate*, so you need to examine each associate degree program carefully before enrolling. For example, some courses emphasize real estate broker training or appraisal training rather than real estate salesperson training. Other programs are designed for people who are already licensed as real estate professionals who are seeking continuing training to advance their careers.

The courses required for a real estate major in a typical associate degree training program are listed below to give you an idea of what you can expect to find in a similar training program near you. This is a program that leads to an associate of applied science degree in real estate at a two-year college in Southern California. The program is designed to serve the needs of students who plan to enter the real estate field, and for students who want to gain additional knowledge of the real estate field after they experience working in the field. The number of real estate credit hours needed to complete the degree ranges from 24 to 29, depending upon the specific concentration (Real Estate General, Real Estate Appraiser, and Mortgage Broker). State residents pay $332 in tuition and fees per year. Non-residents of California pay $2,852 in tuition and fees per year.

Associate of Applied Science Degree
Real Estate General Courses Required for the Major

Course Title	Number of Credit Hours
Real Estate Principles	3
Real Estate Finance	3
Real Estate Appraisal	3

and ONE of the following options:

Legal Aspects of Real Estate	4
Real Estate Practice	4

and ONE of the following:

Real Estate Economics	3
Principles of Accounting	3

and TWO of the following:

Selected Problems in Real Estate Law	3
Real Estate Finance II	3
Real Estate Exchange and Taxation	3
Real Estate Office Administration	3
Real Property Management	3
Real Estate Syndication	3
Real Estate Investment	3
Principles of Escrow	3
Mortgage Loan Brokering and Lending	3
Real Estate Appraisal II	3
Business Law	3

Total Credits Required for Major	**24**
Total Credits Required for Degree	**60**

Since real estate courses make up only 24 of the required 60 credit hours, you may be wondering what the other 36 credit hours consist of. The courses that make up the rest of the degree total outside of your major normally will consist of a mixture of electives and required courses. The ratio of this mixture varies among schools. You'll most likely be required to take a variety of general education courses in fields such as English, science, social science, mathematics, and communications. You may be able to choose electives from any field you want, or you may be restricted to business-related courses in a real estate major associate degree program. All of these options are clearly spelled out in each school's college catalog, so be sure to carefully read the catalogs of the schools you are considering.

Bachelor's Degrees

The bachelor degree program combines courses in a specific major with general education courses in a four-year curriculum at a college or university. You may be admitted to your major program as a freshman or after one or two years of general education or liberal arts courses at another institution. There are several types of bachelor's degrees available—the most common are the bachelor of arts and the bachelor of science. The bachelor of science degree with a major in business/real estate has traditionally been pursued by people who are planning a career in a specialized area of real estate, such as commercial sales, property management, or mortgage brokerage. However, many more residential real estate salespeople are now obtaining a college degree than in years past.

It's a highly personal choice to decide what training program is right for you, so don't be put off from getting a bachelor's degree in real estate just because many entry-level residential real estate sales agents don't have one. If you plan to advance in your career up to the level of broker or specialize in an area of real estate such as finance, commercial, investments, or property management, then a bachelor's degree in real estate would be a big plus. See below for some examples of courses you might take for a bachelor's degree in real estate. This list does not include all the courses required for a bachelor's degree, but will give you an idea of what type of courses are required for a major in real estate.

These courses are offered at a private university in Texas where annual tuition is approximately $9,478. The courses offer students specialized training in real estate appraisal, real estate finance, investment analysis of income-producing property, real estate law, and property management. All the major real estate courses offered at this private university have been approved by the Texas Real Estate License Law to satisfy the state's 45-hour pre-licensing course requirement.

Bachelor of Science Degree	
Real Estate Courses Required for Major	
Course Title	Number of Credit Hours
Real Estate Principles and Practices	3
Real Estate Law	3
Real Estate Appraisal	3
Real Estate Investments	3
Real Estate Finance	3
Real Estate Management	3
Special Studies in Real Estate	1–6
Business Course Electives	3–6
Total Credits Required for Major	**27**
Total Credits Required for Degree	**124**

The courses that make up the rest of the degree total outside of your major will consist of a mixture of electives and required courses. As with the associate degree, the ratio of this mixture varies among schools. However, for a bachelor's degree you'll most likely be required to take a variety of general education courses in fields such as natural sciences, social sciences, mathematics, history, English, fine arts, and communications. You'll also have several elective courses to choose from, many in the business and finance fields. All of these options are clearly spelled out in each school's college catalog, so read carefully the catalogs of the schools you are considering.

The entrance requirements are more competitive for a bachelor's degree program than for shorter training programs. A high school diploma or its equivalent (GED) is required for admission, and placement exams, satisfactory SAT and ACT scores, a high-quality writing sample, positive references, and an acceptable high school GPA may be required. While the requirements for getting into and graduating from a bachelor's degree program may be difficult, the rewards that result from a college degree may make it worthwhile. You have to analyze your current financial situation along with your future goals to figure out if a college degree is necessary for you. The trend in real estate is that more and more entry-level property managers and appraisers hold a college degree; however, many real estate salespeople do not. Before you make a final decision on what length and type of program is right for you, be sure to read chapter four about financial aid. You don't want lack of funds to stop you from pursuing a college degree. Perhaps you can afford more college training than you think.

Another route that some real estate professionals take is to obtain a certificate or an associate degree in real estate and then pursue a bachelor's degree through distance learning while they are working full-time. Distance learning offers greater flexibility than the traditional way of getting an education—attending classes on a college campus or in a professional school.

Distance Training Programs

A growing number of programs are available that are designed for students to earn a degree while working full or part time. Better yet, you never have to go to class! Several colleges and universities now have programs with names like *Degrees at a Distance, Correspondence Courses,* or *Long Distance Learning* that allow you to study and take courses on your own, without attending formal classes.

Distance learning is basically independent study. It focuses on the idea that adults, through their jobs, personal activities, and general life experience, have many of the tools necessary to be successful, independent learners. Generally, they have organizational and time management skills, basic writing and communication skills, and lots of motivation and initiative, and they tend to make serious commitments to their education. If you already have some work and life experience behind you, and believe you are a good candidate for independent study, this could be an excellent way to get the real estate education you need. This also can be a good option for working real estate professionals to complete their associate or bachelor's degrees, or to get additional training. Check with the schools you're interested in to find out if they offer any real estate distance learning programs. You should also contact your state's real estate commission, licensing law office, or appraisal board (listed in Appendix A) to find out if self-study courses are an option for you to fulfill the pre-licensing or continuing education requirements. You can check Appendix B to find names of books that offer additional information about distance learning programs.

CHOOSING THE TRAINING PROGRAM THAT'S BEST FOR YOU

Since there are so many different training programs, it can be a challenge to find the one that is best for you. The first step is to find out which schools in your local area offer real estate training or other college courses that will help you land a job in real estate. The next step is to contact those schools for more information. You should always confirm that each school currently offers courses that are related to real estate. Ask to speak to a guidance counselor or to someone in the real estate or business department to get detailed information about the real estate programs that are offered by each school. Request a school catalog and whatever brochures that are available about the school and its programs. Read these documents carefully when you receive them, especially the fine print in the college catalog. You want to find out exactly what courses are required for your program, how much the program will cost, and how long the program will last.

Another thing you can do, if you have the time, is to visit the schools in your area and talk to a guidance counselor in person at each one. These counselors are trained to help you identify your needs and decide if their school will meet those needs. Follow these steps when preparing for an on-campus visit:

* Contact the office of admissions to request an appointment to visit. Remember to ask for the name of the person making the appointment and the person you will be meeting with. Try to schedule a meeting with an instructor in the real estate program as well as a guidance counselor in the admissions or counseling department.
* Carry with you a copy of your high school transcript and record of any completed college courses if you will have the opportunity to meet with an admission counselor during your visit.
* Create and bring with you a list of honors or awards you have received in high school, another career field, or the community.

Be prepared to ask questions about the school and surrounding community, including extracurricular activities, work opportunities, and anything else you don't find explained in the promotional brochures.

Asking the Right Questions

After you visit several schools and narrow your choices down to two or three schools, the next step is to ask tough questions about each program so you can make the final selection. Here are some important questions you should ask about a prospective school to see if it measures up to your standards. After each question, you'll find sample answers that you should receive or other considerations that you should look for in a prospective school before selecting it as your first choice.

What requirements will I need to attend?

Check with each school that you are considering to find out what its specific entrance requirements are. Requirements vary from school to school. For instance, you may be required to do any one or more of the following:

- Take English, math, or science placement tests
- Take and achieve a certain score on the SAT or ACT if you have not already taken them in high school
- Have a certain level GPA from high school
- Provide proof of immunization
- Write a personal essay stating why you are seeking admission
- Provide the names and phone numbers for three or more personal references

If you feel that you won't have any trouble meeting the entrance requirements for your targeted schools, then you're all set. If one of the schools you are considering has an entrance requirement that you think you may not meet, call an admissions counselor and discuss your particular case with her or him. For educational requirements, many schools will at least offer some type of remedial help if needed, so students can meet the requirement in the future.

What are the qualifications of the faculty?

There should be some faculty members with advanced degrees (M.A., M.S., M.B.A, Ph.D., and so on) or faculty members who have extensive experience as real estate professionals and instructors. In a four-year college or university, you can expect the majority of professors to hold advanced degrees. In shorter programs, such as a certificate program or individual courses, you'll find more instructors who are currently practicing as real estate professionals. In all types of schools, however, the faculty should be accessible to students for individual conferences or meetings when necessary.

Is the school accredited?

It's important that the school you choose be accredited. Accreditation is a rigorous and complex process that ensures sound educational and ethical business practices at the schools that achieve accreditation. It's a process schools undergo voluntarily.

Some accrediting agencies are national and some are regional. The name of the accrediting agency for the school you're interested in will probably be plainly printed on the school's general catalogue because most schools are proud of their accredited status. If you can't locate the information in a school's printed materials, call the school and asking for the name(s) of its accrediting agency or agencies. See Appendix A for contact information for several national and regional accrediting agencies.

An important point to remember is that if the school you choose is not accredited, then you cannot get financial aid through any of the government programs. (See chapter four for more information on how to obtain financial aid.)

What will the program cost?

Tuition varies according to many factors but especially according to the length of the program and the area in which the school is located. Often, tuition costs also depend on if you are a resident of the state in which you are applying for school. You should take some time to figure out how much each program that you are considering will cost. If the tuition is not listed in the college's course catalog, call the school and ask what its current resident and non-resident rates are (depending on whether you are a state resident or not). As you can see from the tuition costs listed in the sample programs above (certificate, associate, and bachelor's), there is quite a range of costs for completing a training program.

Don't forget to include the following items when figuring out how much each school will cost: books, admission fees, lab fees, rent, transportation, and child care. If one school is located near where you live, you may be able to save money on parking and gasoline by walking or taking a bus. Perhaps one school has lower-priced child care or cheaper admission fees. After you create an estimate of the total costs for each school you are considering, you'll be armed with one more item that can make or break a school's desirability for you.

Can I get tuition reimbursement for this program?

Some real estate schools offer you a list of sponsoring real estate companies that are willing to reimburse you for costs of the real estate course if you agree to sign on with their company as a salesperson. Often, the reimbursement will take place after you close your first sale with that company. Schools that have been in business a long time or that have good management may offer this service. It's definitely worth looking into. See chapter four for additional information about tuition reimbursement programs.

What is the student-teacher ratio?

The student-teacher ratio is a statistic that shows the average number of students assigned to one teacher in a classroom. It's important that the student-teacher ratio not be too high. Education suffers if classrooms are too crowded, or if a teacher has too many students to be able to see everyone who wishes to be seen for a private conference. According to one of the top national accrediting agencies, the Accrediting Council for Independent Colleges and Schools, a reasonable student-teacher ratio for skills training is 30 students to 1 teacher in a lecture setting and 15 students to 1 teacher in a laboratory or clinical instruction setting. At very good schools the ratio is even better than the ACICS recommends.

When are classes scheduled?

Find out if the school you're considering offers any weekend or evening classes. If you are working full time during regular business hours while attending school, you'll need to find a school that offers classes at non-traditional times.

Is the campus environment suitable?

When you visit the school, determine how the campus feels to you. Is it too big? Too small? Too quiet? Is the campus in a bustling city or rural community? Is it easily accessible? Do you need to rely on public transportation to get there? Select a school that has a campus environment that meets your needs.

Does the school offer child care facilities?

This may or may not be of concern to you. If it is, you'll want to tour the child care facilities and interview the people who work in the child care center to see if the care is suitable for your children.

Application Tips from Admissions Directors

- Apply as early as you can. You'll need to fill out an application and submit high school or GED transcripts and any copies of SAT, ACT, or other test scores used for admission. If you haven't taken these tests, you may have to before you can be admitted. Call the school and find out when the next program starts, then apply at least a month or two prior to make sure you can complete requirements before the program begins.

- You may receive a pre-written request for high school transcripts from the admissions office when you get your application. Make sure you send those requests as soon as possible, so the admissions process is not held up in any way.

- Make an appointment as soon as possible to take any placement tests that may be required.

- Pay your fees before the deadline. Enrollment is not complete each quarter or semester until you have paid all fees by the date specified on your registration form. If fees are not paid by the deadline, your classes may be canceled. If you are going to receive financial aid, apply as early as you can.

- Find out if you must pass a physical or provide any medical history forms such as immunization records early in the application process, so this does not hold up your admission.

HOW TO GET LICENSED AS A REAL ESTATE PROFESSIONAL

The real estate profession has several licenses, certifications, and professional designations for you to work toward. Whether you want to become a sales agent, broker, appraiser, or other type of real estate professional, rest assured that there are one or more licensing or certification requirements to meet. The first hurdle to pass over for sales agents and brokers is obtaining your real estate sales or broker license.

Sales/Broker License Requirements

You must have a license issued by your state if you want to become a sales agent or broker. Since licenses are controlled at the state level, each state sets its own requirements for granting a license. Here are some examples of what you need to do to get a license in various states:

Salesperson's license in a western state:

1. Education: Complete a 45 classroom hour course in Real Estate Principles
2. Age: Must be at least 18 years old to obtain license
3. Experience: None required
4. Pay: Licensing fee
5. License: Must pass the state exam with 70% or more correct on 150 questions
6. Past: Have fingerprint card completed for background check
7. Activation: License must be activated within one year from date of examination

Salesperson's license in a southern state:

1. Be 18 years of age or older
2. Have a high school diploma or certificate of equivalency
3. Show proof of successful completion of 90 classroom hours of real estate education or its equivalent approved by the Commission
4. Pass the real estate licensing examination administered by the national testing service currently under contract with the Commission
5. Comply with application procedures as required by the Commission's licensing and testing divisions

Broker's License in a western state:

1. Must be 18 years of age or older
2. Proof of legal U.S. residence is required
3. License applicants must be honest and truthful. Conviction of a crime which is either a felony or involves moral turpitude may result in denial of a license
4. Must have successfully completed the following statutorily required college-level courses: (Real Estate Practice, Legal Aspects of Real Estate, Real Estate Finance, Real Estate Appraisal, Real Estate Economics or Accounting) and three courses from the following group: (Real Estate Principles, Business Law, Property Management, Escrows, Real Estate Office Administration, Mortgage Loan Brokering and Lending, Advanced Legal Aspects of Real Estate, Advanced Real Estate Finance, Advanced Real Estate Appraisal)
5. A minimum of two years full-time licensed salesperson experience within the last five years or the equivalent is required
6. Must pass the licensure examination
7. Must pay the applicable fee

Broker's license in a southern state:

1. Must be 18 years of age or older
2. Successfully complete 90 classroom hours of real estate education of which 30 classroom hours must be in basic broker courses, from an accredited postsecondary school or a school or organization licensed by the State Board of Private Career Education within 36 months immediately preceding the date of the application
3. Must have been licensed as an active real estate salesperson or broker for a period of not less than 24 months within the previous 48-month period immediately preceding the date of application—may be waived under certain circumstances
4. Must pass the state license examination
5. Must send the proper forms and fees to the Real Estate Commission no later than 90 days after passing the examination

Since each state has different requirements, the first thing to do is to contact the real estate commission in the state in which you want to get your license to find out what their requirements are. It's important that you get licensed in the state in which you want to work, since not all states accept other states' licensing procedures. For example, if you get licensed as a salesperson in Alabama and then move to California, you may find that you have to start the whole licensing process over, using the guidelines of California's rules. This has historically been the case, although some states are now voting to accept other states' real estate licenses.

Just as the requirements for getting a license vary by each state, so do the actual licensing exams. Four national exams are used by most states.

Taking the Sales/Broker License Exam

The real estate licensing exam is nothing to fear. It is a standardized exam for which you can study and prepare for ahead of time. Several methods of preparation are available to you. Indeed, many of the pre-licensing courses contain material that you will need to know to pass the exam. In addition to the formal real estate courses you take, you can also prepare by studying on your own with the help of an exam preparation book. Several such books are currently on the market. See Appendix B for title and publisher information.

Each state decides which test to administer, and most states now use one of the national testing services that are available. These testing services may manage the creation of the exam, process the applications for the exam, and proctor, score, and report the results of the exam for the state. Here are the most common testing services and a list of the states that use them at the time of this book's printing. Of course, states may choose to adopt a different test in the future, so it's always best to check with your state's real estate commission or licensing agency to get the most current information.

The Applied Measurement Professionals, Inc. (AMP) National Real Estate Exam is given in the following states:

Alabama	Nebraska
Georgia	North Dakota
Michigan	South Dakota
Missouri	Wyoming
Montana	

The Assessment of Systems, Inc. (ASI) National Real Estate Exam is given in the following states:

Arizona	Kentucky
Arkansas	Massachusetts
Colorado	New Jersey
Delaware	Pennsylvania
District of Columbia	South Carolina
Hawaii	Tennessee
Illinois	Utah
Kansas	Washington

The National Assessment Institute (NAI) National Real Estate Exam is given in the following states:

Idaho	New Mexico
Louisiana	Texas

The Psychological Services, Inc. (PSI) National Real Estate Exam is given in the following states:

Iowa	Vermont
Maryland	Virginia
Nevada	Wisconsin
New Hampshire	

The following states do not use any of the national testing services to administer their real estate exam. The exam is prepared by a state agency or staff:

California	Ohio
Florida	Oklahoma
Maine	Oregon
North Carolina	West Virginia

Passing scores vary depending on the state in which you take the exam. For example, in Texas, you can pass the broker license exam with a score of 70, but in Montana, you need a score of 80 to pass. The percentage of people who pass the licensing exam also varies among states. For instance, only 45% of applicants passed the broker license exam who took the test during one year in Hawaii, but over 82% of the applicants passed the broker license exam in Georgia during that same year. If you don't pass the license exam on your first try, don't despair, because you are not alone. The key is to set aside time every day to study and review the most important items that will appear on the test.

Pass the Licensing Exam on Your First Try

Once you've decided to take the licensing exam, you'll need to set up a plan for how to pass it. Several things can help your chances of scoring high on a state licensing exam. Here are a few of them:

◆ Get an idea of what will be on the exam. You can ask people who have already taken the exam what areas were emphasized and what books they recommend you study to prepare for the exam. You may be able to get old tests that have been published for students to review relevant material.

◆ Set priorities on what material to study. You can't possibly learn every detail about the job you want to obtain, so focus on the most important aspects. If you don't, you can easily get bogged down in wading through details that are not going to be tested on the exam.

◆ Study test preparation books to find out or brush up on the skills needed to succeed on written exams. Look up information on how to handle test anxiety, how to find clues for answering multiple-choice questions, and how to take tests within specific time limits. See Appendix B under *Test Preparation* for books relevant to real estate exams.

◆ Make a study schedule several weeks or months before the exam and stick to it. Allow sufficient time each day for studying a section of material and don't forget to preview and review the material you study each day. A good study method is to create flash cards and test yourself on key concepts and questions you think may appear on the test.

◆ Try studying with a partner to boost your chances of getting a passing score. If you know someone who is also taking the same exam, ask him or her to study with you. Ask each other questions and discuss the separate topic areas thoroughly a few hours each week for a month or two before the exam. Or have a friend quiz you on real estate terms or laws.

The test you take in your state will probably include questions about both national and state real estate laws and information. Most tests have a separate section for national and state issues, and the national portion of the exam is normally longer. A portion of the questions will require you to perform basic math computations related to real estate transactions. Here are a couple of sample questions that you might find on a typical broker or salesperson license exam:

Sample Questions

1. Real estate is defined as
   a. land only
   b. land and buildings
   c. land and all permanent attachments to it
   d. land and everything growing on it

2. A broker listed a house in San Francisco for $350,000, at a 6% commission. He later sold the house for $325,000. How much less was the broker's commission on the actual selling price of the home than it would have been on the original listed price?
   a. $1200
   b. $1500
   c. $1600
   d. $1800

3. The United States government insures or guarantees the following types of mortgage loans:
   a. VA loans
   b. conventional loans
   c. private party loans
   d. all of the above

The answers to these sample questions are: 1. c, 2. b, 3. a. Since the exams follow the multiple choice format, you should practice answering these types of questions. Several strategies exist for working with multiple choice questions. Again, pick up a test preparation book and browse through it. See what areas you need the most help with and focus on those. Try to find out as much as possible before you take the exam. Read all materials you get from the state licensing agency or real estate commission carefully. If you aren't sure about any aspect of the test, call to get more information. In fact, you should be armed with a list of questions to ask before you take your exam.

Questions to Ask Before Taking Your Exam

1. How can I register for the exam?

2. How soon can I take the exam?

3. How much does the exam cost?

4. Where can I take the exam?

5. What identification do I need to bring to the exam?

6. What can I bring to the testing site? (i.e., calculator, pencils, scratch paper)

7. What is the passing score for this exam?

8. How long will it take to find out my score?

Real Estate Appraiser Licensing and Certification

The process is quite a bit different for getting licensed as a real estate appraiser than for getting licensed as a real estate salesperson. The appraisal license differs dramatically from the salesperson license because you don't get your license until *after* you have job experience as an appraiser. Of course, you need to get the salesperson license *before* you perform any job duties.

The first step is to contact your state's appraisal board or licensing agency to find out what their requirements are for licensing and certification—see Appendix A for a list of state agencies. Some states offer information about becoming an appraisal trainee. Here's a sample of license requirements in a southern state to give you an idea of what you might find:

Appraiser's license in southern state:

1. Must register as an appraisal trainee

2. Must posses a high school diploma or GED

3. Must complete 90 hours of approved real estate appraisal courses

4. Must be sponsored by an experienced real estate appraiser

5. Must show evidence of completing at least 2,000 hours of appraisal job experience over a minimum of two years

In addition to appraisal *licenses*, you can also get *certified* as an appraiser. Most states offer two different types of real estate appraiser certification exams: residential and general. Residential certification is sought by appraisers who appraise single- to four-family homes, whereas general certification is sought by appraisers who appraise income-producing properties and land in addition to residential properties.

You can contact the appraisal board in your state to find out exactly what requirements they have for becoming certified as a residential or commercial appraiser. Most states require an amount of education and experience that is based on federal standards. You normally need to complete several education courses and possess a certain number of hours of experience in the field before you can even register to take the residential or general certification exam. Here's a sample of one state's requirements; you'll find that many states have the same requirements: Appraiser's residential certification in southern state:

1. Must possess high school diploma or GED
2. Must complete 120 classroom hours of appraisal education
3. Must show evidence of 2,500 hours of appraisal experience conducted in a minimum of two years

Appraiser's general certification in southern state:

1. Must possess high school diploma or GED
2. Must complete 180 classroom hours of appraisal education
3. Must show evidence of 3,000 hours of appraisal experience conducted in a minimum of two and a half years

Residential Certification Exam

Residential certification exams are normally shorter and simpler than the general certification exams. You'll be tested on real estate valuation and appraisal principles and terminology as they relate to residential properties. You will also need to thoroughly understand the standard valuation processes, use appraisal math (such as calculating percentages, means, and rates), and apply legal principles on the exam.

General Certification Exam

The general certification is considered the advanced or level-two exam in real estate appraisal. You will be expected to know everything that is covered on the residential real estate exam *plus* a whole host of additional material related to income-producing properties and land. The test questions will be of a higher level of difficulty and will be more complex in the general certification exam than in the residential one. Areas that are tested on the general certification test include income approach to appraisal, capitalization techniques, compound interest principles, operating statement ratios, and leasehold valuation.

Sample Test Questions

1. How many square feet are there in one acre of land?
   a. 41,600
   b. 43,000
   c. 43,500
   d. 43,560

2. What does an appraiser do?
   a. estimates price
   b. estimates value
   c. determines price
   d. guards value

The answers to the sample questions are 1. d, 2. b. Again, the questions will be in a multiple-choice format, and there are test preparation books that you can use to help you prepare for and pass the appraiser certification exams. With dedication and determination, you can pass your license or certification exam.

Who:	Jack Fidure
What:	Owner of American Select Realty
Where:	Clearwater, Florida
How long:	One year as owner of American Select Realty; five years in the real estate field

Insider's Advice

Real estate sales is a great field to get into if you are an energetic self-starter. After you graduate from high school, you can attend approximately 80 hours of mandatory training, get your real estate sales license and be well on your way to making good money, all within a matter of a couple of months. I know real estate agents who are making $500,000–$600,000 a year selling residential real estate. How else can you make that kind of money so quickly? In addition, the prospects for the future remain positive because real estate is such an integral part of life. People will always be buying and selling property, and the real estate professionals who are strong will survive.

Another benefit to having a career in the real estate field is that sales agents are not locked into any one real estate company. If they don't like how one particular office is being run, it's not mandatory that they stay there. They have the flexibility to find a new office with different guidelines and rules. The only downfall to breaking into real estate sales is the financial uncertainty at the beginning. It may take four to six months to see a commission check, so you need to have some other income or savings to sustain you through those first few months.

Insider's Take on the Future

My company does 50% sales and 50% property management for both residential and commercial properties. The compensation for property management is more steady than income from sales, but it is usually quite a bit lower per property. So the more properties you manage, the higher your monthly income. A standard commission for property managers is approximately 10–15% of the amount of the rent.

We have been investing in advertising since we're a new company. Most of the people who own the property we manage do not live in Florida, so a lot of our advertising appears in large cities such as New York, Chicago, and Boston. Advertising one's services successfully is a major factor in growth, so we have a significant mix of outlets: a Web Page on the Internet, printed advertisements in several cities, billboards, and of course, the Yellow Pages.

CHAPTER 3

This chapter contains a directory of proprietary and career schools, independent and community colleges, and public and private universities that offer real estate training courses. All programs provide school name, address, and phone number, so you can contact each school directly to get more information and application forms for their real estate training programs.

DIRECTORY OF REAL ESTATE TRAINING PROGRAMS

Now that you've decided to get into a training program, you need to find one at a school near you. Whether you've decided that you want to complete the minimum number of courses needed to get your sales license or to obtain a bachelor's degree in real estate, you'll find relevant schools in this chapter. The schools are listed in alphabetical order by city within each state, so you can quickly locate schools in whatever city you intend to work. While the specific schools included in this chapter are not endorsed or recommended by LearningExpress, they are intended to help you begin your search for an appropriate school by offering a representative listing of accredited or state-approved schools in each state. Since there are so many schools that offer real estate training programs, not all of the schools in the country could be listed here due to space limitations. However, this representative listing should get you started. The training programs these schools offer range from a 45 hour course to a certificate to an associate degree to a bachelor's degree and beyond. Therefore, you should contact each school to find out exactly what type of real estate training they offer.

For additional information on real estate training programs, see Appendix A for the names and contact information of state real estate licensing agencies. You can contact the agency in your state to request a list of real estate schools that they have approved.

ALABAMA
Jefferson State Community College
2601 Carson Road
Birmingham 35215
205-853-1200

John C. Calhoun State Community College
P. O. Box 2216
Decatur 35609-2216
205-306-2500

Enterprise State Junior College
Enterprise 36331-1300
334-347-2623

Wallace State Community College
801 Main Street Northwest
Hanceville 35077-2000
205-352-8278

Alabama Institute of Real Estate
3938B Government Boulevard, Suite 101
Mobile 36693
334-666-6765

Alabama Real Estate Institute, Inc.
2426 Spruce Street
Montgomery 36107
205-262-2701

Chattahoochee Valley State Community College
Phoenix City 36869-7928
334-291-4928

Northeast Alabama State Community College
P. O. Box 159, Highway 35 West
Rainsville 35986-0159
205-638-4418

University of Alabama
P. O. Box 870132
Tuscaloosa 35487-0132
205-348-5666

ALASKA
Commonwealth School of Real Estate
4105 Turnagain Boulevard
Anchorage 99517
907-248-1717

University of Alaska
3211 Providence Drive
Anchorage 99508
907-786-1800

ARIZONA
Arizona Institute of Real Estate
2310 North Fourth Street
Flagstaff 86004
602-526-6091

Ford Schools
4425 Olive Avenue
Glendale 85302
602-249-3221

Glendale Community College
6000 West Olive Avenue
Glendale 85302-3090
602-435-3305

Mohave Community College
1971 Jagerson Avenue
Kingman 86401
520-757-0898

Mesa Community College
1833 West Southern Avenue
Mesa 85202-4866
602-461-7000

Bud Crawley Real Estate School
4621 North 16th Street, Suite B201
Phoenix 85016
602-263-0090

Paradise Valley Community College
18401 North 32nd Street
Phoenix 85032
602-493-2610

Phoenix College
1202 West Thomas Road
Phoenix 85013
602-264-2492

Professional Institute of Real Estate
10207 North Scottsdale Road
Scottsdale 85253
602-991-0182

Scottsdale Community College
9000 East Chaparral Road
Scottsdale 85250-2699
602-423-6100

Arizona College of Real Estate
421 East Bartow
Sierra Vista 85635
602-459-5770

Arizona State University, Main Campus
Box 870112
Tempe 85287-0112
602-965-9011

Brodsky School of Real Estate
720 South Craycroft Road
Tucson 85711
602-747-1485

Hogan School of Real Estate
4023 East Grant Road
Tucson 85712
602-327-6849

Pima Community College
4905 East Broadway Boulevard
Tucson 85709-1010
520-748-4640

ARKANSAS

Arkansas-Oklahoma School of Real
Estate
2201 Dodson Avenue
Fort Smith 72901
501-782-1236

Arkansas State University
P. O. Box 1630
Jonesboro 72467-1630
800-382-3030

ERA Collins School of Real Estate
10201 West Markham, Suite 306
Little Rock 72205
501-224-2212

National Real Estate School
5323 John F. Kennedy Boulevard
North Little Rock 72116
501-753-1633

Real Estate Education Center
3418 West Sunset, Suite E
P. O. Box 6686
Springdale 72762
501-750-2772

CALIFORNIA

Mercury Real Estate Schools
1775 East Lincoln Avenue
Anaheim 92805
714-778-3305

Cabrillo College
Aptos 95003-3194
408-479-6201

Manna Institute
18832 Norwalk Boulevard
Artesia 90701
213-402-4520

West Coast Schools
5385 El Camino Real
Atascadero 93422
805-466-7843

Bakersfield College
1801 Panorama Drive
Bakersfield 93305-1299
805-395-4316

Barstow College
2700 Barstow Road
Barstow 92311-6699
619-252-2411

Mulhearn Licensing School
16911 Bellflower Boulevard
Bellflower 90706
310-866-0719

California State University,
Dominguez Hills
1000 East Victoria Street
Carson 90747-0001
310-243-3645

Southwestern College
900 Otay Lakes Road
Chula Vista 91910
619-421-6700

West Hills Community College
300 Cherry Lane
Coaling 93210
209-935-0801

Compton Community College
1111 East Artesia Boulevard
Compton 90221-5393
310-637-2660

West Los Angeles College
4800 Freshman Drive
Culver City 90230-3500
310-287-4246

DeAnza College
21250 Stevens Creek Boulevard
Cupertino 95014
408-864-5678

Cuyamaca College
El Cajon 92019-4304
619-670-1980

Metropolitan Collegiate Institute
16661 Ventura Boulevard, Suite 518
Encino 91436
818-990-3100

College of the Redwoods
Eureka 95501-9300
707-445-6722

Anthony Schools of Foster City
1065 East Hillsdale Boulevard,
Suite 112
Foster City 94404-1614
415-570-2284

Coastline Community College
11460 Warner Avenue
Fountain Valley 92708
714-546-7600

Ohlone College
43600 Mission Boulevard
Fremont 94539
510-659-6202

California State University, Fresno
5241 North Maple Avenue
Fresno 93740
209-278-2191

Fresno City College
1101 East University Avenue
Fresno 93741-0002
209-442-8240

Fullerton College
321 East Chapman Avenue
Fullerton 92632-2095
714-992-7000

Exacta Schools
12812 Valley View, Suite 12
Garden Grove 92645
714-898-9547

Rainbow Real Estate School
8342 Garden Grove Boulevard, Suite 6
Garden Grove 92644
714-636-9340

Gavilan College
5055 Santa Teresa Boulevard
Gilroy 95020
408-848-4735

Glendale Community College
1500 North Verdugo Road
Glendale 91208-2894
818-240-1000

Citrus College
Glendora 91741-1899
818-914-8517

Miller School of Real Estate
17050 Chatsworth Street, Suite 115
Granada Hills 91344
818-368-4206

California State University, Hayward
Hayward 94542-3000
510-881-3817

Chabot College
25555 Hesperian Boulevard
Hayward 94545
510-786-6700

Golden West College
Huntington Beach 92647-2748
714-895-8121

Imperial Valley College
380 East Aten Road
P. O. Box 158
Imperial 92251-0158
619-352-8320

College of Marin
Kentfield 94904
415-485-9417

Allied Real Estate Schools
22952 Alcalde Drive, Suite 15
Laguna Hills 92653
800-542-5543

Antelope Valley College
3041 West Avenue K
Lancaster 93534-5426
805-943-3241

California State University-Long Beach
1250 Bellflower Boulevard
Long Beach 90840-0106
310-985-5471

Long Beach City College
4901 East Carson Street
Long Beach 90808
562-938-4205

Foothill College
12345 El Monte Road
Los Altos Hills 94022-4599
415-949-7517

California Association of Realtors®
525 S. Virgil Avenue
Los Angeles 90020
213-739-8200

California State University, Los Angeles
5151 State University Drive
Los Angeles 90032
213-343-3888

Los Angeles City College
855 North Vermont Avenue
Los Angeles 90029-3590
213-953-4381

Los Angeles Southwest College
1600 West Imperial Highway
Los Angeles 90047-4810
213-241-5320

Los Angeles Trade-Technical College
400 West Washington Boulevard
Los Angeles 90015-4108
213-744-9420

University of Southern California
University Park
Los Angeles 90089-0911
213-740-6364

Yuba College
2088 North Beale Road
Marysville 95901-7699
916-741-6705

Merced College
3600 M Street
Merced 95348-2898
209-384-6187

Saddleback College
Marguerite Parkway
Mission Viejo 92692-3697
714-582-4555

Academy of Real Estate Professionals
2909 Coffee Road, Suite 4
Modesto 95355
209-522-2842

Modesto Junior College
435 College Avenue
Modesto 95350-5800
209-575-6470

Monterey Peninsula College
Monterey 93940-4799
408-646-4006

East Los Angeles College
1301 Cesar Chavez Avenue
Monterey Park 91754-6001
213-265-8966

Napa Valley College
2277 Napa Vallejo Highway
Napa 94558-6236
707-253-3000

California Academy of Real Estate
18817 Napa Street
Northridge 91324
818-885-7828

California State University, Northridge
18111 Nordhoff Street
Northridge 91330-0001
818-885-3777

Cerritos College
Norwalk 90650-6298
310-860-2451

California School of Real Estate
7971 Capwell Drive, Suite 300
Oakland 94621
510-635-9084

Merritt College
12500 Campus Drive
Oakland 94619-3196
510-466-7369

Mira Costa College
1 Barnard Drive
Oceanside 92056-3899
619-757-2121

Butte College
3536 Butte Campus Drive
Oroville 95965-8399
916-895-2511

Oxnard College
4000 South Rose Avenue
Oxnard 93033-6699
805-986-5843

College of the Desert
43-500 Monterey Avenue
Palm Desert 92260-9305
760-346-8041

California State Polytechnic University,
Pomona
3801 West Temple Avenue
Pomona 91768-4019
909-869-2000

Herbert Hawkins Real Estate School
230 North Lake Avenue
Pasadena 91101
818-795-8871

Pasadena City College
1570 East Colorado Boulevard
Pasadena 91106-2041
818-578-7397

Preferred School of Real Estate
230 N. Lake Avenue
Pasadena 91108
818-795-9811

Los Medanos College
Pittsburg 94565-5197
510-439-2181

Diablo Valley College
321 Golf Club Road
Pleasant Hill 94523-1544
510-685-1230

Porterville College
100 East College Avenue
Porterville 93257
209-791-2313

Chaffey College
5885 Haven Avenue
Rancho Cucamonga
909-987-1737

Shasta College
P. O. Box 496006
Redding 96049-6006
916-225-4841

Riverside Community College
Riverside 92506-1293
909-222-8615

Sierra College
5000 Rocklin Road
Rocklin 95677-3397
916-624-3333

American River College
4700 College Oak Drive
Sacramento 95841-4286
916-484-8375

Browning Real Estate School
2 Sandhill Court
Sacramento 95831
916-399-1416

California State University
6000 J Street
Sacramento 95819-6048
916-278-7362

Cosumnes River College
8401 Center Parkway
Sacramento 95823-5799
916-688-7410

Sacramento City College
3835 Freeport Boulevard
Sacramento 95822-1386
916-558-2438

Hartnell College
156 Homestead Avenue
Salinas 93901
408-755-6700

Realty Institute
2086 South E Street
San Bernadino 92408
909-872-1933

San Bernadino Valley College
San Bernadino 92410-2748
909-888-6511

San Diego City College
1313 Twelfth Avenue
San Diego 92101-4787
619-230-2470

San Diego Mesa College
San Diego 92111-4998
619-627-2682

San Diego Mirimar College
10440 Black Mountain Road
San Diego 92126-2999
619-536-7854

San Diego State University
5300 Campanile Drive
San Diego 92182-8080
619-594-6871

City College of San Francisco
50 Phelan Avenue
San Francisco 94112-1821
415-239-3291

San Francisco State University
1600 Holloway Avenue
San Francisco 94132
415-338-2164

Mt. San Jacinto College
San Jacinto 92583-2399
909-487-6752

Evergreen Valley College
3095 Yerba Buena Road
San Jose 95135-1598
408-270-6441

San Jose City College
2100 Moorpark Avenue
San Jose 95128-2797
408-288-3707

Cuesta College
P. O. Box 8106
San Luis Obispo 93403
805-546-3100

Palomar College
1140 West Mission
San Marcos 92069-1487
619-744-1150

College of San Mateo
1700 West Hillsdale Boulevard
San Mateo 94402
415-574-6161

Contra Costa Colleg
San Pablo 94806-3195
510-235-7800

Century 21 West Division
1851 E. First Street
Santa Ana 92705
800-394-2121

Rancho Santiago College
1530 West 17th Street
Santa Ana 92706-3398
714-564-6053

Santa Barbara City College
721 Cliff Drive
Santa Barbara 93109
805-965-0581

Mission College
300 Mission College Boulevard
Santa Clara 95054-1897
408-988-2200

Allan Hancock College
800 South College Drive
Santa Marias 93454-6399
805-922-6966

Santa Monica College
1900 Pico Boulevard
Santa Monica 90405-1644
310-452-9220

Santa Rosa Junior College
1501 Mendocino Avenue
Santa Rosa 95401-4395
707-527-4011

West Valley College
14000 Fruitvale Avenue
Saratoga 95070
408-741-2001

Columbia College
1160 Columbia College Drive
Sonora 95370
209-533-5100

Lake Tahoe Community College
One College Drive
South Lake Tahoe 96150-4524
916-541-4660

San Joaquin Delta College
5151 Pacific Avenue
Stockton 95207
209-474-5051

Solano County Community College
District
4000 Suisun Valley Road
Suisum 94585
707-864-7000

Lassen Community College
P. O. Box 3000
Susanville 96130
916-257-6181

Los Angeles Mission College
Sylmar 91342-3200
818-364-7658

El Camino College
16007 Crenshaw Boulevard
Torrance 90506-0001
310-660-3567

Mendocino College
P. O. Box 3000
Ukiah 95482-0300
707-468-3103

Ventura College
Ventura 93003-3899
805-654-6455

Victor Valley College
Victorville 92392-5849
619-245-4271

College of the Sequoias
915 South Mooney Boulevard
Visalia 93277
209-730-3727

San Joaquin Delta College
8400 West Mineral King Avenue
Visalia 93291-9283
209-651-2500

Mount San Antonio College
1100 North Grand Avenue
Walnut 91789-1399
909-594-5611

College of the Siskiyous
800 College Avenue
Weed 96094
916-938-5215

Rio Hondo College
3600 Workman Mill Road
Whittier 90601-1699
310-692-0921

Los Angeles Harbor College
Wilmington 90744-2311
310-522-8318

Los Angeles Pierce College
6201 Winnetka Avenue
Woodland Hills 91371
818-347-0551

West Valley Occupational Center
6200 Winnetka Avenue
Woodland Hills 91367
818-346-3540

Los Angeles Valley College
5800 Fulton Avenue
Van Nuys 91401
818-781-1200

All Valley Real Estate School
1248 Franklin Road
Yuba City 95991
916-671-9171

Crafton Hills College
11711 Sand Canyon Road
Yucaipa 92399-1799
909-389-3372

COLORADO
University of Colorado
Campus Box 178
Boulder 80309
800-331-2801

Century 21 Academy Real Estate School
3520 Galley Road, Suite 200
Colorado Springs 80909
719-574-9701

Jones Real Estate College
1919 North Union Boulevard
Colorado Springs 80909
719-473-0385

Pikes Peak Community College
6913 Gayle Lyn Lane
Colorado Springs 80919
800-456-6847

All Service Real Estate Academy
1190 South Colorado Boulevard
Denver 80222
303-757-0021

Colorado Real Estate Institute
1780 South Bellaire Street, Suite 222
Denver 80222
303-744-1363

Metropolitan State College
Campus Box 75 - Box 173362
Denver 80217-3362
303-556-3058

University of Denver
University Park, MRB 107
Denver 80208
303-871-2036

Colorado State University
Fort Collins 80523-0015
970-491-6909

Morgan Community College
17800 Road 20
Ft. Morgan 80701
800-622-0216

Colorado Mountain College
215 Ninth Street
Glenwood Springs 81602
800-621-8559

Aims Community College
5401 West 29th Street
Greeley 80631
303-330-8008

Colorado Association of Realtors Real
Estate School
309 Inverness Way South
Inglewood 80112
303-790-7099

Jefferson County Association of Realtors
Education Training Center
950 Wadsworth Boulevard
Lakewood 80215
303-233-7831

Red Rocks Community College
13300 West Sixth Avenue
Lakewood 80228-1255
303-986-6160

Arapahoe Community College
2500 West College Drive
Littleton 80160-9002
303-797-5970

Northeastern Junior College
100 College Drive
Sterling 80751
303-522-6600

A. J. Educational Services, Inc.
2930 West 72nd Avenue
Westminster 80030
303-426-6443

CONNECTICUT
Connecticut Association of Realtors
111 Founders Plaza, Suite 1101
East Hartford 06108
860-290-6601

Manchester Community-Technical
College
Manchester 06045-1046
860-647-6050

Real Estate Career Institute, Inc.
894 South Main Street
P. O. Box 1025
Southington 06489
203-628-0373

University of Connecticut
2131 Hillside Road
Storrs 06269-3088
203-486-2000

DELAWARE
Delaware School of Real Estate
7234 Lancaster Pike, Suite 200
Hockessin 19707
302-656-4457

DISTRICT OF COLUMBIA
American University
440 Massachusetts Avenue Northwest
Washington 20016
202-885-6000

George Washington University
2121 I Street, Suite 102
Washington 20052
202-994-6040

FLORIDA
South Florida Community College
600 West College Drive
Avon Park 33825
813-453-6661

Florida Atlantic University
777 Glades Road
P. O. Box 3091
Boca Raton 33431-0991
561-367-2758

Brevard Community College
1519 Clear Lake Road
Cocoa 32922-6597
407-632-1111

University of Miami
Coral Gables 33124
305-284-4323

Broward Community College
225 East Las Olas Boulevard
Ft. Lauderdale 33301
305-761-7465

University of Florida
West University Avenue and 13th Street
Gainesville 32611
352-392-1365

Florida Community College at
Jacksonville
501 West State Street
Jacksonville 32202-4030
904-632-3110

University of North Florida
4567 St. Johns Bluff Road South
Jacksonville 32224-2645
904-646-2703

Okaloosa-Walton Community College
College Boulevard
Niceville 32578-1295
904-729-5223

Valencia Community College
P. O. Box 3028
Orlando 32802-3028
407-299-5000

Gulf Coast Community College
5230 West Highway 98
Panama City 32401-1058
904-769-1551

Bob Hogue School of Real Estate
5531 Ninth Street North
St. Petersburg 33703
813-526-5338

Florida State University
Tallahassee 32306-1009
904-644-6200

GEORGIA
Georgia Institute of Real Estate
3341 Lexington Road
Athens 30605
706-549-6400

University of Georgia
Athens 30602
706-542-2112

Barney Fletcher School
Atlanta Institute of Real Estate
3200 Professional Parkway
Galleria 75, Suite 275
Atlanta 30339
404-850-9090

Georgia State University
University Plaza
519 One Park Place South
Atlanta 30303
404-651-2365

Morehouse College
830 Westview Drive Southwest
Atlanta 30314
404-215-2632

Augusta State University
2500 Walton Way
Augusta 30904-2200
706-737-1401

Meybohm Institute of Real Estate
2848 Washington Road
Augusta 30909
706-736-2281

Real Estate Training Institute
527 Newnan Street
Carrollton 30017
404-836-0042

West Georgia College
Maple Street
Carrollton 30118
404-836-6500

Middle Georgia College
Sarah Street
Cochran 31014
912-934-6221

Bob Wood Real Estate School
468 Beaver Ruin Road
Norcross 30071
404-449-4410

HAWAII
Fahrni School of Real Estate
98-277 Kamehameha Highway
Aiea 96701
808-486-8444

Hawaii Institute of Real Estate
841 Bishop Street, Room B11
Honolulu 96813
808-521-0071

University of Hawaii - Manoa
2600 Campus Road, Room 001
Honolulu 96822
808-956-8975

IDAHO
Idaho Association of REALTORS®
1450 West Bannock
Boise 83702-5294
208-342-3585

Idaho Real Estate Education Council
633 North Fourth Street
P. O. Box 83720
Boise 83720-0077
208-334-3285

Eastern Idaho Technical College
1600 South 2500 East
Idaho Falls 83404-5788
208-524-3000

Lewis-Clark State College
Eighth Avenue and Sixth Avenue
Lewiston 83501-2698
208-746-2341

University of Idaho
Moscow 83844
800-422-6013

Northwest Nazarene College
Nampa 83651
208-467-8011

Idaho State University
Pocatello 83209
208-236-4000

College of Southern Idaho
315 Falls Avenue
P. O. Box 1238
Twin Falls 83303-1238
208-733-9554

ILLINOIS
Illinois Academy of Real Estate
316 North Lake Street #2
Aurora 60506
630-844-0222

Belleville Area College
2500 Carlyle Road
Belleville 62221-5899
618-235-2700

Berth & Associates Real Estate Academy
275 West Dundee Road
Buffalo Grove 60089
708-541-8100

Real Estate Institute of America
343 Torrence
Calumet City 60409
708-891-2202

Parkland College
Champaign 61821-1899
217-351-2482

City Colleges of Chicago
Harold Washington College
30 East Lake Street
Chicago 60601
312-553-5600

City Colleges of Chicago
Kennedy-King College
6800 South Wentworth Avenue
Chicago 60621
312-602-5502

City Colleges of Chicago
Olive-Harvey College
10001 South Woodlawn Avenue
Chicago 60628
312-291-6380

National Real Estate School
6321 North Avondale Avenue
Chicago 60631
312-763-4241

Realtors Real Estate School
520 North Michigan Avenue, Suite 1300
Chicago 60611
312-222-4910

Robert Morris College
180 N. LaSalle Street
Chicago 60601
800-225-1520

Prairie State College
202 South Halsted Street
Chicago Heights 60411
312-709-3516

Morton College
3801 South Central Avenue
Cicero 60650
708-656-8000

McHenry County College
8900 U. S. Highway 14
Crystal Lake 60012-2761
815-455-8716

Danville Area Community College
2000 East Main Street
Danville 61832-5199
217-443-8800

Illinois Academy of Real Estate
Tom Brinkoetter Company
1698 East Pershing Road
Decatur 62526
217-875-0555

Richland Community College
One College Park
Decatur 62521
217-875-7200

Oakton Community College
Des Plaines 60016-1268
847-635-1703

Sauk Valley Community College
173 Illinois Route 2
Dixon 61021-9110
815-288-5511

Illinois Central College
One College Drive
East Peoria 61635-0001
309-694-5353

Elgin Community College
Elgin 60123-7193
847-888-7385

Northwestern University
1801 Hinman Avenue
P. O. Box 3060
Evanston 60204-3060
847-491-7271

Carl Sandburg College
Galesville 61401-9576
309-344-2518

College of DuPage
Lambert Road and 22nd Street
Glen Ellyn 60137
630-942-2441

Illinois Association of Realtors
1368 D'adrian Professional Pike
Godfrey 62035-1120
618-466-0022

Lewis and Clark Community College
5800 Godfrey Road
Godfrey 62035
618-467-2222

College of Lake Country
19351 West Washington Street
Grayslake 60030-1198
847-223-6601

Southeastern Illinois College
3575 College Road
Harrisburg 62946
618-252-6376

Zittel School of Real Estate
4950 North Harlem Avenue
Harwood Heights 60656
708-867-5757

Joliet Junior College
Joliet 60431-8938
815-729-9020

Kankakee Community College
P. O. Box 888
Kankakee 60901-0888
815-933-0345

Real Estate Training, Inc.
1700 Ogden Avenue
Lisle 60532
708-960-3700

Kishwaukee College
Malta 60150
815-825-2086

Black Hawk College, Moline
Moline 61265-5899
309-796-1311

Mars School of Real Estate Education
4363 North Harlem Avenue
Norridge 60634
708-457-2000

Coldwell Banker Institute of Real Estate
1211 West 22nd Street, Suite 700
Oakbrook 60523
630-218-2815

Dabbs Academy of Real Estate
15567 South 94th Avenue
Oakland Park 60462
708-535-5540

William Rainey Harper College
Palatine 60067-7398
847-925-6247

Triton College
River Grove 60171-9983
708-456-0300

Rock Valley College
3301 North Mulford Road
Rockford 61114
815-654-4250

Center for Real Estate Studies
3701 West Algonquin Road
Rolling Meadows 60008
800-236-8371

Institute for Development of Sales
Potential, Inc.
1645 Hicks, Suite L
Rolling Meadows 60008
847-349-2625

Terry Schiro & Associates Real Estate
Academy
1732 West Wise Road
Schaumberg 60193
708-980-2363

South Suburban College
South Holland 60473-1270
708-596-2000

Lincoln Land Community College
Springfield 62794-9256
217-786-2243

Ronald D. Ladley and Company
National Academy of Real Estate
1999 Wabash Avenue, Suite 205
Springfield 62704
217-525-6677

Waubonsee Community College
Route 47 at Harter Road
Sugar Grove 60554-0901
708-466-4811

Illinois University of Urbana-Champaign
506 South Wright Street
Urbana 61801
217-333-0302

INDIANA
Indiana University - Bloomington
Bloomington 47405
812-855-0661

Ivy Technical State College - Northeast
3800 North Anthony Boulevard
Fort Wayne 46805
219-482-9171

Indiana University - Purdue
425 University Boulevard, CA129
Indianapolis 46202-5143
317-274-4591

Vincennes University
Jasper Campus
Jasper 47546-9393
812-482-3030

Ball State University
Muncie 47306
317-285-8300

IOWA

Center for Professional and Executive
Development
102 English Office Building
Ames 50011-2081
515-294-8967

Iowa Real Estate School of Cedar
Rapids
385 Collins Road, Northeast
Cedar Rapids 52402
319-393-4900

Key Real Estate School
501 South Main
Council Bluffs 51503
712-328-3133

Iowa Association of Realtors
999 Oakridge Drive
Des Moines 50314
515-244-2295

Iowa Lakes Community College
Estherville 51334-2295
712-362-2604

Western Iowa Technical Community
College
4647 Stone Avenue
Sioux City 51102
712-275-6400

Coldwell Banker Mid-America
Group of Real Estate
4800 Westown Parkway
West Des Moines 50266
515-224-8787

KANSAS

Dodge City Community College
Dodge City 67801-2399
316-225-1321

Butler County Community College
El Dorado 67042-3280
316-321-2222

Independence Community College
Brookside Drive and College Avenue
P. O. Box 708
Independence 67301-0708
316-331-4100

Real Estate School of Kansas City
5210 Northeast Chouteau Trafficway
Kansas City 64119-2509
816-453-3826

Haskell Indian Junior College
155 Indian Avenue, #1282
Lawrence 66046
913-749-8454

Real Estate School of Lawrence
P. O. Box 3271
Lawrence 66046
913-843-1309

Topeka Institute of Real Estate
5120 West 28th
Topeka 66614-2399
913-273-1330

Wichita State University
1845 Fairmount Drive
Wichita 67208-1595
316-689-3085

KENTUCKY

Ashland Community College
1400 College Drive
Ashland 41101-3683
606-329-2999

Elizabethtown Community College
College Street Road
Elizabethtown 42701
502-769-2371

Lexington Community College
Oswald Building, Cooper Drive
Lexington 40506-0235
606-257-6066

Realtors Institute
161 Prosperous Place
Lexington 40509
606-263-7377

Family Style School of Professional
Licensing
7711 Beulah Church Road
Louisville 40228
502-968-2241

Jefferson Community College
109 East Broadway
Louisville 40202-2005
502-584-0181

Madisonville Community College
Madisonville 42431-9185
502-821-2250

Paducah Community College
P. O. Box 7380
Paducah 42002-7380
502-554-9200

Prestonburg Community College
One Bert T. Combs Drive
Prestonburg 41653-9502
606-886-3863

Eastern Kentucky University
Lancaster Avenue
Richmond 40475-3101
606-622-1000

LOUISIANA

Louisiana Realtors Association
P. O. Box 14780
Baton Rouge 70898
504-923-2210 or 800-272-8392

Louisiana State University and
Agriculture and Mechanical College
Baton Rouge 70803-3101
504-388-3202

Louisiana Technical College
Sullivan Campus
1710 Sullivan Drive
Bogalusa 70427
504-732-6640

First Professional School of Real Estate
4200 South I-10 Service Road West,
Suite 134
Metairie 70001
800-966-9866

Louisiana Technical College
Jefferson Campus
5200 Blair Drive
Metairie 70001
504-736-7072

Northeast Louisiana University
Monroe 71209
318-342-5252

University of New Orleans
Lake Front
New Orleans 70148
504-286-6000

Baker's Professional Real Estate College
1612 Fairfield Avenue
Shreveport 71101
318-222-7459

Louisiana Technical College
Shreveport Bossier Campus
P. O. Box 78527
2010 North Market
Shreveport 71107
318-676-7811

MAINE

University of Southern Maine
37 College Avenue
Gorham 04038
800-800-4876

University of Maine at Machias
Machias 04654-1321
207-255-3313

Casco Bay College
477 Congress Street
Portland 04101-3483
207-772-0196

Thomas College
180 West River Road
Waterville 04901-5097
800-339-7001

MARYLAND

Champion Institute of Real Estate
2560 Riva Road
Annapolis 21401
410-544-6004

Anne Arundel Community College
101 College Parkway
Arnold 21012-1895
410-647-7100

Harford Community College
401 Thomas Run Road
Bel Air 21015
410-836-4223

Weichert Real Estate School
6610 Rockledge Drive, Suite 100
Bethesda 20817
301-718-4143

Nyman Academy of Real Estate
4933 Allentown Road
Camp Springs 20746
301-449-3315

Catonsville Community College
800 South Rolling Road
Catonsville 21228
410-455-4304

O'Brien Institute of Real Estate
Route 5, P. O. Box 584
Charlotte Hall 20622
301-855-6700

The Columbia Academy of Real Estate
9186 Carriage House Lane
Columbia 21045
410-964-2860

Pro Real Estate Academy
9300 Livingston Road
Fort Washington 20744
301-248-3502

Long & Foster Institute of Real Estate
200 Orchard Ridge Drive
Gaithersburg 20878
301-417-7100

Maryland School of Real Estate
7 Park Avenue
Gaithersburg 20877
301-984-9700

Century 21 Real Estate School
849 International Drive
P. O. Box 2048
Glen Burnie 21061
410-766-5850

Diplomat Real Estate Center
5505 Sargent Road
Hyattsville 20782
301-559-6000

Champion Institute of Real Estate
541B Baltimore-Annapolis Boulevard
Severna Park 21146
410-544-6004

Villa Julie College
Green Spring Valley Road
Stevenson 21153
410-486-7001

Champion Institute of Real Estate
411 Thompson Creek
Stevensville 21619
410-643-7454

Montgomery College
Takoma Park Campus
Takoma Park 20912
301-650-1493

O'Conor, Piper & Flynn School of Real
Estate
22 West Padonia Road Training Center
Timonium 21093
410-252-2111

Farrall Institute
P. O. Box 40
Waldorf 20604
301-645-1700

MASSACHUSETTS
Northeastern University
360 Huntington Avenue
Boston 02115
617-437-2000

Smith-McLaughlin-Hart Real Estate
School
195 State Street
Boston 02109
617-742-3900

Massachusetts Institute of Technology
Center for Real Estate
77 Massachusetts Avenue
Cambridge 02139
617-253-4791

Nichols College
Center Road
P. O. Box 5000
Dudley 01571
800-470-3379

Greenfield Community College
1 College Drive
Greenfield 01301-9739
413-774-3131

Northern Essex Community College
Haverhill 01830
508-374-3605

Real Estate Salesman School
580 Appleton Street
Holyoke 01040
413-532-1418

Sullivan Real Estate School
Sullivan Building, Route 132
Hyannis 02601
508-775-1433

Greater Springfield Association of
Realtors School
221 Industry Avenue
P. O. Box 4826
Springfield 01101
413-785-1328

American Real Estate Academy
771 Main Street
Waltham 21540
617-893-2832

MICHIGAN
Ferris State University
901 South State Street
Big Rapids 49307
616-592-2000

Henry Ford Community College
5101 Evergreen Road
Dearborn 48128
313-845-9615

Wayne County Community College
801 West Fort Street
Detroit 48226
313-496-2500

U. S. Brokers Institute, Inc.
300 East Beltline Avenue Northeast
Grand Rapids 49506
616-942-6660

Mid-Michigan Community College
1375 South Clare Avenue
Harrison 48625
514-386-6622

Kalamazoo Valley Community College-
Texas Township
6767 West O Avenue
Kalamazoo 49009
616-372-5000

Western Michigan University
Kalamazoo 49008
616-387-2000

Lansing Community College
419 North Capitol Avenue
Lansing 48901-7210
517-483-1957

NCI Associates Ltd.
27637 John Road
Madison Heights 48071
313-548-2090

Currey Management Institute
6875 Rochester Road
Rochester 48306
810-656-0600

Kirtland Community College
10775 North St. Helen Road
Roscommon 48653
517-275-5121

Theresa A. Morse School of Real Estate
20600 Eureka, Suite 422
Taylor 48195
313-284-5110

Century 21 Great Lakes, Inc.
5750 New King Street, Suite 300
Troy 48098
810-641-5000

The Real Estate School
755 West Big Beaver, Suite 1390
Troy 48084
248-269-6333

Delta College
University Center 48710
517-686-9092

MINNESOTA
Itasca Community College
Grand Rapids 55744
218-327-4464

Rainy River Community College
International Falls 56649
218-285-2212

Mankato State University
MSU 55
Mankato 56002-8400
507-389-1822

St. Cloud State University
115 Administrative Services Building
720 Fourth Avenue South
St. Cloud 56301
320-255-2244

Ridgewater College
P. O. Box 1097
Wilmar 56201-1097
320-231-2902

MISSISSIPPI
Delta State University
Cleveland 38733
601-846-4018

University of Southern Mississippi
Box 5166
Hattiesburg 39406
601-266-5000

Mississippi State University
P. O. Box 5268
Mississippi State 39762
601-325-2224

University of Mississippi
Oxford 38677
601-232-5869

Hinds Community College
Raymond 39154-9799
601-276-2000

East Mississippi Community College
P. O. Box 158
Scooba 39358-0158
601-476-8442

Northwest Mississippi Community
College
Senatobia 38666-1701
601-562-3222

MISSOURI
University of Missouri, Columbia
Columbia 65211
573-882-2456

St. Louis Community College
Kirkwood 63122-5720
314-984-7608

Lindenwood College
209 South Kings Highway
St. Charles 63301-1695
314-949-4949

St. Louis Community College at
Florissant Valley
3400 Pershall Road
St. Louis 63135-1499
314-595-4250

Webster University
470 East Lockwood Boulevard
St. Louis 63119-3194
314-968-6991

Drury College
900 North Benton Avenue
Springfield 65802
417-873-7205

Real Estate School of Springfield
306 East Pershing Street
Springfield 65806
417-862-6677

Southwest Missouri State University
901 South National
Springfield 65804-0094
417-836-5517

Thrust International School of Real
Estate
196 Historic 66 East
Waynesville 65583
314-774-5312

MONTANA
Connole-Morton Schools
415 North Higgins Avenue
Missoula 59802
406-543-3269

NEBRASKA
University of Nebraska at Kearney
905 West 25th Street
Kearney 68849-0001
308-865-8441

Larabee School
245 South 84th Street, Suite L101
Lincoln 68510
402-488-8334

The Moore Group
3460 South 17th Street
Lincoln 68502-4807
402-423-8605

Nebraska School of Real Estate
225 North Cotner Boulevard, Suite 106
Lincoln 68505
402-467-1717

Professional School of Real Estate
4645 Normal Boulevard, Suite 105
Lincoln 68506
402-434-3725

Northeast Community College
Norfolk 68702-0469
402-644-0459

Mid-Plains Community College
North Platte 69101-9491
308-532-8740

Metropolitan Community College
P. O. Box 3777
Omaha 68103-0777
402-457-2563

Randall School of Real Estate
11224 Elm Street
Omaha 68144
402-333-3004

University of Nebraska - Omaha
60th and Dodge Street
Omaha 68182
402-554-2393

Western Nebraska Community College
Scottsbluff 69361
308-635-6010

NEVADA
Western Nevada Community College
Carson City 89703-7316
702-887-3138

Americana School of Real Estate
3790 Paradise Road, Suite 200
Las Vegas 89109
702-796-8888

Ellsberg-Williamson School of Real
Estate
2050 South Maryland Parkway, Suite A3
Las Vegas 89109
702-731-5110

Real Estate School of Nevada
4180 South Sandhill Road, Unit B-10
Las Vegas 89121
702-454-1936

Southern Nevada School of Real Estate
3441 West Sahara Avenue, Suite C5
Las Vegas 89102
702-364-2525

University of Nevada, Las Vegas
4505 South Maryland Parkway
Las Vegas 89154
702-895-3443

Community College of Southern
Nevada
North Las Vegas 89030-4296
702-651-4060

Northern Nevada Real Estate School
3951 South McCarren Boulevard
Reno 89502
702-829-1055

Truckee Meadows Community College
Mail Station #15
Reno 89512-3901
702-673-7042

NEW HAMPSHIRE
New Hampshire Technical Institute
Concord 03301-7412
603-225-1863

NEW JERSEY
Camden County College
Blackwood 08012-0200
609-227-7200

Ocean School of Real Estate
586 Route 70
Brick 08723
908-477-4921

M.W. Funk Sales Institute
498 North Kings Highway, Suite 200
Cherry Hill 08034
609-667-0800

Real Estate School of Central New
Jersey
1734 Oak Tree Road
Edison 08820
908-548-0603

Zacharie School of Real Estate
Village Harbour Executive Camp
675 Route 72, Suite 1006A
Manahawkin 08050
609-597-5800

Professional School of Business
22 East Willow Street
Millburn 07041
201-564-8686

Weichert Real Estate School
1625 Route 10 East
Morris Plains 07950
800-544-3000

Kovat's Real Estate and Insurance
School
The Bergen Mall
Paramus 07652
201-843-7277

Burlington County College
Route 530
Pemberton 08068-1599
609-894-9311

Princeton School of Real Estate
238 West Delaware Avenue
Pennington 08534
609-737-1525

Fairleigh Dickenson University
1000 River Road
Teaneck 07666-1996
800-338-8803

Gloucester County College
1400 Tanyard Road
Sewell 08080
609-468-5000

Raritan Valley Community College
P. O. Box 3300
Somerville 08876-1265
908-218-8861

Ocean County College
Toms River 08754-2001
732-255-0304

Thomas Edison State College
101 West State Street
Trenton 08608-1176
609-984-1100

South Jersey Professional School of
Business
2121 Villa Shopping & Professional
Center
Route 73
West Berlin 08091
609-767-0600

NEW MEXICO
New Mexico State University-
Alamogordo
Alamogordo 88310
505-439-3700

New Mexico Real Estate Institute
8205 Spain Road Northeast, Suite 109
Albuquerque 87109
505-821-5556

Clovis Community College
Clovis 88101-8381
505-769-4021

San Juan College
Farmington 87402-4699
505-599-0318

New Mexico Junior College
Hobbs 88240-9123
505-392-5092

New Mexico State University
Box 30001 Dept. 3A
Las Cruses 88003-8001
505-646-3121

University of New Mexico-Valencia
Campus
Los Lunas 87031-7633
505-865-9667

Eastern New Mexico University
Portales 88130
800-367-3668

Sante Fe Community College
Santa Fe 87502-4187
505-438-1262

NEW YORK
State University of New York
College of Technology at Alfred
Alfred 14802-1196
607-587-4215

Queensborough Community College of
the City University of New York
222-05 56th Avenue
Bayside 11364
718-631-6236

Suffolk County Community College-
Western Campus
Brentwood 11717
516-434-6704

City University of New York-Lehman
College
Balford Park Boulevard West
Bronx 10468
718-960-8706

New York Real Estate Institute
407 Avenue P
Brooklyn 11223
718-339-7845

State University of New York
College of Technology at Canton
Canton 13617
315-386-7123

Five Towns College
305 North Servia Road
Dix Hills 11746
516-424-7000

Nassau Community College
1 Education Drive
Garden City 11530-6793
516-572-7345

Columbia-Greene Community College
Hudson 12534-0327
518-828-4181

Cornell University
Field of Real Estate
Ithaca 14853
607-255-5241

Orange County Community College
115 South Street
Middletown 10940
914-314-4030

Borough of Manhattan Community
College
199 Chambers Street
New York 10007-1079
212-346-8101

New York University
22 Washington Square North
New York 10011-9108
212-998-4500

The Sobelsohn School
370 Seventh Avenue
New York 10001
212-244-3900

Suffolk County Community College-
Eastern Campus
Riverhead 11901
516-548-2513

St. John Fisher College
3690 East Avenue
Rochester 14618-3597
716-385-8064

Suffolk County Community College-
Ammerman Campus
Seldon 11784-2851
516-451-4022

Rockland Community College
145 College Road
Suffern 10901-3699
914-574-4237

Hudson Valley Community College
80 Vandenburgh Avenue
Troy 12180
815-270-7309

Mohawk Valley Community College
1101 Sherman Drive
Utica 13501-5394
315-792-5400

Utica School of Commerce
201 Bleeker Street
Utica 13501-2280
315-733-2307

Westchester Community College
Valhalla 10595-1698
914-785-6735

NORTH CAROLINA

Stanley Community College
141 College Drive
Albemarle 28001
704-982-0121

Randolph Community College
P. O. Box 1009
Asheboro 27204
910-633-0200

Appalachian State University
Boone 28608
704-262-2120

Central Piedmont Community College
P. O. Box 35009
Charlotte 28235-5009
704-330-6006

Sampson Community College
P. O. Box 318
Clinton 28328
910-592-8081

Haywood Community College
185 Freedlander Drive
Clyde 28721-9453
704-627-4508

Surry Community College
630 South Main Street
Box 304
Dobson 27017-0304
910-386-8121

Bladen Community College
P. O. Box 266
Dublin 28332
910-862-2164

College of the Albermarle
1208 North Road Street
P. O. Box 2327
Elizabeth City 27906-2327
919-335-0821

Fayetteville Technical Community
College
Fayetteville 28303-0236
910-678-8274

NC Blue Ridge Community College
Flat Rock 28731
704-692-3572

Wayne Community College
Caller Box 8002
Goldsboro 27533-8002
919-735-5151

Alamance Community College
Graham 27253-8000
910-578-2002

East Carolina University
East Fifth Street
Greenville 27858-4553
919-328-6640

Pitt Community College
P. O. Drawer 7007
Greenville 27835-7007
919-321-4245

Catawba Valley Community College
Hickory 28602-9699
704-327-7009

Caldwell Community College and
Technical Institute
2855 Hickory Boulevard
Hudson 28638-2397
704-726-2200

Guilford Technical Community College
Box 309
Jamestown 27282
910-334-4822

Davidson County Community College
P. O. Box 1287
Lexington 27293-1287
910-249-8186

Carteret Community College
3505 Arendell Street
Morehead City 28557
919-247-4142

Western Piedmont Community College
1001 Burkemont Avenue
Morgantown 28655
704-438-6051

Tri-County Community College
2300 Highway 64 East
Murphy 28906
704-837-6810

Craven Community College
800 College Court
New Bern 28562
919-638-4131

Sandhills Community College
2200 Airport Road
Pinehurst 28374
910-695-3738

Wake Technical Community College
Raleigh 27603-5696
919-662-3343

Central Carolina Community College
1105 Kelley Drive
Sanford 27330
919-775-5401

Isothermal Community College
Spindale 28180-0804
704-286-3636

Mayland Community College
Spruce Pine 28777-0547
704-765-7356

Brunswick Community College
Supply 28462-0030
910-754-6900

Southwestern Community College
275 Webster Road
Sylva 28779
704-586-4091

Edgecombe Community College
Tarboro 27886-9399
919-823-5166

Beaufort County Community College
P. O. Box 1069
Washington 27889
919-946-6194

Rockingham Community College
P. O. Box 38
Wentworth 27375-0038
910-342-4261

Cape Fear Community College
411 North Front Street
Wilmington 28401-3393
910-251-5116

Forsyth Technical Community College
Winston-Salem 27103-5197
910-723-0371

NORTH DAKOTA
Bismarck State College
1500 Edwards Avenue
Bismarck 58501
701-224-5400

North Dakota State College of Science
800 North Sixth Street
Wahpeton 58076
800-342-4325

OHIO
Southern Ohio College-Northeast
Campus
2791 Mogadore
Akron 44312-1596
330-733-8766

Northwest State Community College
Archbold 43502-9542
419-267-5511

Kent State University, Ashtabula
Campus
Ashtabula 44004-2299
216-964-4240

University of Cincinnati-Clermont
College
College Drive
Batavia 45103
513-732-5200

Malone College
515 25th Street Northwest
Canton 44709
330-471-8246

Cincinnati State Technical & Community
College
3520 Central Parkway
Cincinnati 45223-2690
513-569-1550

Southern Ohio College, Cincinnati
Campus
Cincinnati 45215
513-771-2424

Southwestern College of Business
Cincinnati 45246-1122
513-874-0432

University of Cincinnati-Access Colleges
100 Edwards Center
Cincinnati 45221-0091
513-556-1100

University of Cincinnati-
Raymond Walters College
9555 Plainfield Road
Cincinnati 45236
513-745-5700

Cuyahoga Community College-
Metropolitan Campus
2900 Community College Avenue
Cleveland 44115-3123
216-987-4030

David Myers College
112 Prospect Avenue
Cleveland 44115-1096
216-696-9000

Dyke College
112 Prospect Avenue
Cleveland 44115
216-523-3800

Columbus State Community College
Box 1609
Columbus 43216-1609
614-227-2669

Franklin University
201 South Grant Avenue
Columbus 43215
614-341-6237

Ohio State University
Columbus Campus
1800 Cannon Drive
Columbus 43210-1200
614-292-3980

Sinclair Community College
444 West Third Street
Dayton 45402-1460
937-226-3060

Lorain County Community College
Elyria 44035
216-365-4191

Terra State Community College
Fremont 43420-9670
419-334-8400

Miami University-Hamilton Campus
1501 Peck Boulevard
Hamilton 45011
513-863-8833

Cuyahoga Community College, Eastern
Campus
4250 Richmond Road
Highland Hills 44122
216-987-2000

Lakeland Community College
7700 Clocktower Drive
Kirtland 44094
216-953-7100

Hocking Technical College
3301 Hocking Parkway
Nelsonville 45764
614-753-3591

Cuyahoga Community College, Western
Campus
Parma 44130-5199
216-987-5154

Edison State Community College
Piqua 45356-9253
937-778-8600

University of Rio Grande
Rio Grande 45674
614-245-5353

Jefferson Community College
4000 Sunset Boulevard
Steubenville 43952
614-264-5591

University of Toledo
2081 West Bancroft
Toledo 43606-3398
419-537-2696

Kent State University, Trumbull Campus
Warren 44483-1998
330-847-0571

OKLAHOMA
Western Oklahoma State College
2801 North Main Street
Altus 73521
405-477-2000

Rogers State College
College Hill Drive
Claremore 74017
918-341-7510

University of Central Oklahoma
Edmond 73034-0172
405-341-2980

University of Oklahoma
660 Parrington Oval
Norman 73019
405-325-2251

Oklahoma City Community College
7777 South May Avenue
Oklahoma City 73159-4419
405-682-7515

University of Tulsa
600 South College Avenue
Tulsa 74104
800-331-3050

OREGON

Foghorn School of Real Estate
17 West Marine Drive
Astoria 97103
503-325-7682

Lane Community College
Eugene 97405-0640
541-747-4501

Oregon Business College
2300 Oakmont Way, Room 106
Eugene 97401
503-484-0784

Real Estate School of Eugene
1142 Willagillespie Road, Suite 34
Eugene 97401
503-485-6205

Real Estate and Insurance Schools of
Oregon
1133 South Riverside Avenue, Suite 8
Medford 97501-7807
541-772-1171

Clackamas Community College
19600 South Molalla Avenue
Oregon City 97045
503-657-8400

Advanced Educational System
10225 Southwest Parkway
Portland 97225
503-297-1344

Century 21 Peninsula School of Real
Estate
8040 North Lombard Street
Portland 97203
503-286-5826

Portland Community College
P. O. 19000
Portland 97280-0990
503-414-2227

Professional Training Institute, Inc.
11959 Southwest Garden Place
Portland 97223
503-624-1509

Professional Trainers
533 Southeast Main
Roseburg 97470
541-672-9200

Century 21 Elite School of Real Estate
58147 South Columbia River Highway
St. Helens 97051
503-397-5023

Center for Professional Studies
1822 Lancaster Drive Northeast
Salem 97305-9730
503-371-4471

Chemeketa Community College
4000 Lancaster Drive NE
Salem 97309-7070
503-399-5006

Norman F. Webb Real Estate Courses
1112 Twelfth Street Southeast
Salem 97302
503-364-0881

PENNSYLVANIA

Northampton County Area Community
College
3825 Green Pond Road
Bethlehem 18017
610-861-5500

Montgomery County Community
College
Blue Bell 19422-0796
215-641-6550

Clarion University of Pennsylvania
Clarion 16214
814-226-2306

Penn State-Erie Behrend College
Station Road
Erie 16563-0195
814-898-6100

University Center at Harrisburg
One HACC Drive
Harrisburg 17110-2999
717-780-2410

Immaculata College
Immaculata 19345-0900
610-647-4400

St. Francis College
P. O. Box 600
Loretto 15940-0600
814-472-3100

Robert Morris College
881 Narrows Run Road
Moon Township 15108-1189
412-262-8206

Luzerne County Community College
Nanticoke 18634-9804
717-740-7336

Bucks County Community College
Newtown 18940-1525
215-968-8119

Community College of Philadelphia
1700 Spring Garden Street
Philadelphia 19130
215-751-8000

Greater Philadelphia Realty Board-Real
Estate School
2010 Rhawn Street
Philadelphia 19152
215-722-3400

Temple University
1801 North Broad Street
Philadelphia 19122-6096
215-204-7200

University of Pennsylvania
1 College Hall
Philadelphia 19104-6376
215-898-7507

Community College of Allegheny
808 Ridge Avenue
Pittsburgh 15233
412-325-6614

Duquesne University
600 Forbes Avenue
Pittsburgh 15282
412-396-6220

University of Pittsburgh
Pittsburgh Campus
Bruce Hall, 2nd Floor
Pittsburgh 15260
412-624-7488

Lehigh Carbon Community College
Schnecksville 18078-2598
610-799-1134

Shippensburg University of
Pennsylvania
Shippensburg 17257
717-532-9121

Westmoreland County Community
College
Youngwood 15697
412-925-4060

RHODE ISLAND
Community College of Rhode Island
Warwick 02886-1807
401-825-2285

SOUTH CAROLINA
South Carolina Institute of Real Estate
10 Diamond Lane
Columbia 29210
803-798-4804

University of South Carolina
Columbia 29208
803-777-7700

Wyatt Institute of Real Estate
710 East North Street
Greenville 29601
803-233-1514

Coastal Carolina University
Myrtle Beach 29578-1954
803-349-2026

Fortune School of Real Estate
P. O. Box 3845
Myrtle Beach 29578
803-236-1131

Orangeburg-Calhoun Technical College
Orangeburg 29118-8299
803-535-1218

SOUTH DAKOTA
LaMont School of Real Estate
P. O. Box 152
Huron 57350
800-503-2121

Dakota West Institute
1719 West Main Street
Rapid City 57701
800-568-6016

Southeast Vocational-Technical Institute
2301 Career Place
Sioux Falls 57107
800-247-0789

University of South Dakota
414 East Clark Street
Vermillion 57069
605-677-5011

Loren Anderson Seminars
122 West Third Street
Yankton 57078
800-657-5892

TENNESSEE
North Central Institute
168 Jack Miller Boulevard
Clarksville 37042
615-552-6200

Jackson State Community College
Jackson 38301-3797
901-425-2644

East Tennessee State University
P. O. Box 70731, ETSU
Johnson City 37614
615-929-4213

Pellissippi State Technical Community
College
P. O. Box 22990
Knoxville 37933-0990
615-694-6400

University of Tennessee, Knoxville
320 Student Services Building
Knoxville 37996-0230
423-974-2184

University of Memphis
159 Administration Building
Memphis 38152
901-678-2111

Middle Tennessee State University
Murfreesboro 37132
615-898-2111

Martin Methodist College
433 West Madison Street
Pulaski 38478
615-363-9868

Motlow State Community College
Tullahoma 37388-8100
615-393-1500

TEXAS
Amarillo College
P. O. Box 447
Amarillo 79178-0001
806-371-5000

University of Texas at Arlington
701 South Nedderman
P. O. Box 19120
Arlington 76019
817-273-2225

Trinity Valley Community College
Athens 75751-2765
903-675-6357

Austin Community College
5930 Middle Fiskville Road
Austin 78752-4390
512-223-7000

Lamar University - Beaumont
P. O. Box 10009
Beaumont 77710
409-880-8888

Bee County College
3800 Charco Road
Beeville 78102
512-358-3130

Blinn College
Brenham 77833-4049
409-830-4140

Panola College
1109 West Panola Street
Carthage 75633
903-693-2037

Cisco Junior College
Cisco 76437-9321
817-442-2567

Texas A&M University
College Station 77843
409-845-3741

Montgomery College
Conroe 77384
713-591-3523

Del Mar College
Baldwin and Ayres
Corpus Christi 78404-3897
512-886-1248

Navarro College
3200 West Seventh Avenue
Corsicana 75110-4899
903-874-6501

Richland College
Dallas 75243-2199
972-238-6100

Southern Methodist University
P. O. Box 296
Dallas 75275
214-768-2058

Grayson County College
Denison 75020-8299
903-463-8650

University of North Texas
P. O. Box 13797
Denton 76203
817-565-2681

El Paso Community College
P. O. Box 20500
El Paso 7998-0500
915-594-2150

University of Texas at El Paso
500 West University Avenue
El Paso 79968-0001
915-747-5588

Tarrant County Junior College
1500 Houston Street
Fort Worth 76102
817-336-7851

Texas Christian University
TCU Box 297020
Fort Worth 76129
817-921-7490

North Central Texas College
Gainesville 76240-4699
817-668-7731

Hill College of the Hill Junior College
District
Hillsboro 76645-0619
817-582-5555

Champion School of Real Estate
3724 FM1960 West, Suite 116
Houston 77068
713-893-4484

Houston Community College System
P. O. Box 7849
Houston 77270-7849
713-718-8615

North Harris Montgomery Community
College District
250 North Sam Houston Parkway East
Houston 77060
713-443-5400

San Jacinto College-North Campus
Houston 77049-4599
281-458-4050

San Jacinto College-South Campus
Houston 77089-6099
281-922-3431

Spencer School of Real Estate
1700 El Camino Real
Houston 77058
713-480-7711

North Lake College
Irving 75038-3899
972-273-3109

Schreiner College
2100 Memorial Boulevard
Kerrville 78028
800-343-4919

Kilgore College
Kilgore 75662-3299
903-983-8200

Central Texas College
P. O. Box 1800
Killeen 76542-4199
817-526-1104

Laredo Community College
West End Washington Street
Laredo 78040-4395
210-721-5177

South Plains College
Levelland 79336-6595
806-894-9611

Angelina College
P. O. Box 1768
Lufkin 75902-1768
409-633-5212

Collin County Community College
2200 West University Drive
McKinney 75069
214-548-6710

Northeast Texas Community College
Mount Pleasant 75456-1307
903-572-1911

Lamar University - Orange
Orange 77630-5899
409-883-7750

Paris Junior College
Paris 75460-6298
903-784-9431

San Jacinto College-Central Campus
Pasadena 77501-2007
281-476-1819

Angelo State University
2601 West Avenue N
San Angelo 76909
915-942-2042

St. Philips College
1801 Martin Luther King Drive
San Antonio 78203
210-531-4831

Temple College
2600 South First Street
Temple 76504-7435
817-298-8282

Texarkana College
2500 North Robison Road
Texarkana 75599-0001
903-838-4541

College of the Mainland
1200 Amburn Road
Texas City 77591-2499
409-938-1211

Tyler Junior College
Tyler 75711-9020
903-510-2399

Victoria College
2200 East Red River
Victoria 77901-4494
512-572-6407

Baylor University
P. O. Box 97056
Waco 76798
800-229-5678

McLennan Community College
1400 College Drive
Waco 76708-1499
817-299-8657

UTAH
Utah Valley State College
1200 South 800 West
Orem 84058
801-222-8000

Brigham Young University
Provo 84602
801-378-6489

O'Brien Schools
575 East 4500 South
Salt Lake City 84107
801-266-5613

Salt Lake Community College
4600 South Redwood Road
P. O. Box 30808
Salt Lake City 84130-0808
801-957-4297

Stringham Real Estate School, Inc.
5248 South Pinemont Drive, #C250
Salt Lake City 84123
801-269-8889

Wardley Real Estate School
205 West 700 South, Suite 201
Salt Lake City 84101
801-533-8378

VIRGINIA
Northern Virginia Community College
8333 Little River Turnpike
Annandale 22003-3796
703-985-8483

Piedmont Virginia Community College
501 College Drive
Charlottesville 22902-8714
804-977-3900

John Tyler Community College
13101 Jefferson Davis Highway
Chester 23831-5399
804-796-4000

Eastern Shore Community College
29300 Lankford Highway
Melfa 23410
757-787-5913

Alpha College of Real Estate
11861 Canon Boulevard, Suite A
Newport News 23606
757-873-1079

Christopher Newport University
50 Shoe Lane
Newport News 23606-2998
804-594-7100

Tidewater Community College
7000 College Drive
Portsmouth 23703
804-484-2121

Southwest Virginia Community College
Box 5UCC
Richlands 24641-1510
540-964-2555

J. Sargeant Reynolds Community
College
P. O. Box 85622
Richmond 23285-5622
804-371-3029

Moseley-Flint School of Real Estate
7206 Hull Street Road
Richmond 23235
804-276-7974

University of Richmond
Richmond 23173
800-700-1662

Virginia Commonwealth University
821 West Franklin Street, Box 2526
Richmond 23284-9005
804-828-1200

Moseley-Flint School of Real Estate
1727 Peters Creek Road
Roanoke 24017
703-562-2575

Coldwell Banker Institute of Real Estate
1953 Gallows Road, Suite 175
Vienna 22180
703-556-6100

Alpha Omega College of Real Estate
2697 International Parkway
Parkway 4, Suite 180
Virginia Beach 23452
757-427-1740

Wytheville Community College
Wytheville 24382-3308
540-223-4755

WASHINGTON

Green River Community College
12401 Southeast 320th Street
Auburn 98092-3699
206-833-9111

Bellevue Community College
Bellevue 98007-6484
206-641-2222

Whatcom Community College
Bellingham 98226-8003
360-676-2170

Olympic College
Bremerton 98337-1699
360-478-4542

Lower Columbia College
Longview 98632-0310
360-577-2304

Columbia Basin College
Pasco 99301-3397
509-547-0511

Peninsula College
Port Angeles 98362-2779
360-417-6230

Renton Technical College
3000 Northeast Fourth Street
Renton 98056-4195
206-235-5840

Century 21 Real Estate Academy
1800 International Boulevard, Suite 1021
Seattle 98188
206-248-2100

North Seattle Community College
9600 College Way North
Seattle 98103-3599
206-527-3773

Shoreline Community College
16101 Greenwood Avenue North
Seattle 98133
206-546-4621

Spokane Falls Community College
3410 West Fort George Wright Drive
Spokane 99224-5288
509-533-3520

Pierce College
9401 Farwest Drive Southwest
Tacoma 98498
206-964-6500

Clark College
Vancouver 98663-3598
360-992-2392

Yakima Valley Community College
P. O. Box 1647
Yakima 98907
509-574-4752

WEST VIRGINIA
Davis and Elkins College
Elkins 26241-3996
800-624-3157

Fairmont State College
Fairmont 26554
800-641-5678

Marshall University
400 Hal Greer Boulevard
Huntington 25755-2020
304-696-3160

WISCONSIN
Chippewa Valley Technical College
620 West Clairemont Avenue
Eau Claire 54701-6120
715-833-6246

Madison Area Technical College
3550 Anderson Street
Madison 53704-2599
608-246-6212

University of Wisconsin - Madison
750 University Avenue
Madison 53706
608-262-3961

Milwaukee Area Technical College
700 West State Street
Milwaukee 53233-1443
414-297-6301

Robbins & Lloyd School of Real Estate and Insurance
5309 North 118th Court
Milwaukee 53225
414-464-0800

University of Wisconsin - Milwaukee
P. O. Box 413
Milwaukee 53201
414-229-3800

Waukesha County Technical College
Pewaukee 53072-4601
414-691-5271

Nicolet Area Technical College
Rhinelander 54501-0518
715-365-4451

Wauwatosa Real Estate Institute, Inc.
11622 West North Avenue
Wauwatosa 53226
414-476-7979

WYOMING
Tom Ostlund Seminars
3704 Carey Avenue
Cheyenne 82001
307-634-4244

Academy Real Estate School
P. O. Box 6444
Rock Springs 82901
307-382-8801

Who:	Chester Baumgartner
What:	Commercial Real Estate Sales Agent/Broker
Where:	Southwest Florida
How long:	Four years

Insider's Advice

Commercial real estate sales is a challenging career. It's really a people business that centers around sales. If you are a good salesperson and enjoy working with people, you can do very well. I succeeded because I did what I said I would do, and acted in a professional manner with all my customers and clients. While the commissions are much higher than in residential real estate (for example, a $50,000 commission is not unusual), you just don't know when they will come through. The deals take a long time to come to fruition and many obstacles lie in the path of a deal's closing. It takes patience and perseverance to build up a business and get a strong network of contacts in your area of specialization. Most agents do specialize in one area because there is so much to learn and know about each type of commercial property. I specialized in selling small industrial buildings, such as mom-and-pop machinery businesses and fabrication buildings. Other agents specialize in areas such as leasing, mobile home parks, shopping centers, businesses, foreclosures, land, and so on.

You can learn about commercial real estate by first becoming a residential sales agent to get the basics down, and then branching out into the commercial arena, or you can go to college to study commercial real estate principles. I didn't have specific commercial real estate training, other than what was needed to pass the agent/broker licensing exam. They just gave me a phone book and said jump in. I got to know people in the field by contacting them and talking with them about their businesses, and gradually built up a business. Once I was involved in commercial sales, I took self-study courses toward earning the professional designation Certified Commercial Investment Member (CCIM), which is conferred by the Commercial Investment Real Estate Institute (CIREI). They offer helpful courses, and I won a scholarship for the first year. So the information is out there to help you succeed in commercial real estate, if you have motivation and can sustain yourself through the often lean early months.

Insider's Take on the Future

I started out in upscale residential sales, and when the company I worked for opened a commercial division, I moved into that area. I loved working in commercial real estate sales. But after four years in the business, I made a career change and am no longer actively selling commercial real estate. However, I do regularly renew my broker/salesperson license because it is not an easy license to obtain. The renewal process is very streamlined and organized. I fulfill the mandatory continuing education requirements through self-study courses. The real estate industry seems to be moving in the direction of seeking out serious and professional agents who are dedicated to the field. So if you have good sales and communication skills, and can market yourself effectively, you can achieve success in commercial real estate.

CHAPTER | 4

This chapter covers how to receive financial aid for the training program you want to attend. You'll find out how to determine your eligibility for financial aid, distinguish among the different types of aid, gather your financial records, and file your forms once you have completed them. A sample financial aid form is included.

FINANCIAL AID FOR THE TRAINING YOU NEED

Now that you have decided that building a career in real estate is what you want to do, and you have chosen a training program, you need a plan for financing your training. That is what this chapter is all about. You can qualify for aid at several different types of schools, including community colleges, technical colleges, universities, and vocational schools that offer short-term training programs, certificates, associate degrees, and bachelor's degrees. You can often qualify for some type of financial aid even if you're attending only part time. The financial aid you'll get may be less than in full-time programs, but it can still be worthwhile and help you pay for a portion of your real estate training program.

Before diving into the world of financial aid, you should first determine if you can get your real estate training for free, so to speak. While this option may not be available in every state or for every real estate career, it's definitely worth looking into.

TUITION REIMBURSEMENT FOR SALESPEOPLE

What better form of financial aid could you find than getting your entire tuition for a training program reimbursed? Yes, it does sound enticing—so what's the catch? The catch is not usually all that painful, thankfully. In fact, the catch is often a job offer written in cement. That is, a particular real estate company reimburses you the cost of a real estate sales course if you agree to work for that company for a set number of months or until you close your first sale. Of course, you'll have to dig around to find real estate companies that are willing to do this, and not all are. However, if you find one that does, this route can be a good option for getting your training for free.

Another way to find real estate companies that are willing to reimburse you for the basic pre-licensing education real estate courses is directly from the real estate schools that you are considering attending. For instance, the Bob Hogue School of Real Estate, Inc. located in Tampa Bay, Florida sends prospective students a list of approximately 100 real estate companies that offer the 100% tuition reimbursement program to students who choose to work for them after graduation. That's an exciting proposition, especially since the list includes such a variety of real estate companies, including national franchises and independent companies in several locations.

Keep in mind though, that these offers are usually only geared toward short-term real estate courses that satisfy the pre-licensing education requirement in your state—not the more lengthy real estate associate or bachelor's degree programs. If you are planning to get an associate or bachelor's degree, it may make more sense for you to enroll in your program of study and take the pre-licensing education courses there, so you can get college credit for them. If you do enroll in an associate or bachelor's degree program, a whole new world of financial aid will open up to you.

ENTERING THE WORLD OF FINANCIAL AID

Don't let financial aid anxiety deter you from finding out more about the many options you have for financing your training program. Take a deep breath, relax, and plunge into the world of financial aid knowing that you can get a handle on the whole process during the time it takes you to read this chapter. Of course, you can read guides the size of a phone book that are devoted to financial aid, but you'll get a good overview in the space of this chapter. (Some of those guides are listed at the end of this chapter, so you can consult them for reference.) Additionally, most schools have good financial aid advisors, who can address your concerns and help you fill out the necessary paperwork. So there is no shortage of information available to help you. Take advantage of it today!

Don't be Fooled by Financial Aid Myths

There's a lot of confusion out there about financial aid. You may have heard some of the age-old myths about the whole financial aid process. One of the most common myths is that the red tape involved in finding sources and applying for financial aid is confusing and overwhelming. In reality, however, it's not as confusing as people say it is. The whole financial aid process is a set of steps that are ordered and logical. Besides, several sources of help are available to you. For instance, this chapter will outline the entire process and give you tips on how to get the most financial aid you can. There are also resources at the end of this chapter that you can go to for additional help.

Another common myth is that the financial aid that most students get is only a burdensome loan that takes them heavily into debt, or a job from a work study program that will lead to burn-out and poor grades. But beware, because this is only a myth! The truth is that in addition to federal grants and scholarships, most schools have their own grants and scholarships that the student doesn't have to pay back, and many students get these. You can also get a combination of scholarships, loans, and work-study. It's worth taking out a loan if it means attending the school you really want to attend, rather than settling for second choice or not going to school at all. As for working while in school, it's true it is a challenge to hold down a full-time or even a part-time job while in school, but a small amount of work-study employment while attending classes (10–12 hours per week) actually improves academic performance because it forces students to increase their time-management skills.

This last myth is really about the terminology of the financial aid process. It goes something like this: I can't understand the financial aid process because of all the unfamiliar terms and strange acronyms that are used. At first glance, this myth sounds believable; however, it too can be exposed for what it really is: a false belief. While you will encounter an amazing number of acronyms and some unfamiliar terms while applying for federal financial aid, as you progress through the process, these acronyms will actually become quite familiar to you. You'll probably find yourself spouting them off when you meet with a financial aid counselor before you're through with the whole process. For additional help in deciphering this maze of terms, you can refer to the handy acronyms key and glossary at the end of this chapter for quick definitions and clear explanations of the most commonly used terms and acronyms.

ARE YOU ELIGIBLE FOR FINANCIAL AID?

To receive federal financial aid from an accredited college or institution's student aid program, you must:

- have a high school diploma or a General Education Development (GED) certificate, pass a test approved by the U. S. Department of Education, or meet other standards your state establishes that are approved by the U. S. Department of Education
- be enrolled or accepted for enrollment as a regular student working toward a degree or certificate in an eligible program
- be a U. S. citizen or eligible non-citizen possessing a social security number. Refer to Immigration and Naturalization Service (INS) in the section entitled *Resources* that appears at the end of this chapter if you are not a U.S. citizen and are unsure of your eligibility
- have a valid social security number
- make satisfactory academic progress
- sign a statement of educational purpose and a certification statement on overpayment and default
- register with selective services, if required
- have financial need, except for some loan and other aid programs

You are eligible to apply for federal financial aid by completing the FAFSA even if you haven't yet been accepted or enrolled in a school. However, you do need to be enrolled in an accredited training program in order to actually receive any funds from a federal financial aid program.

How Do You Get Started?

The first step in beginning the financial aid process is to get a form that is called *Free Application for Federal Student Aid* (FAFSA). You can get this form from several sources: your public library, your school's financial aid office, on-line at http://www.finaid.org/finaid.html, or by calling 1-800-4-FED-AID. You need to get an original form to mail in, however; photocopies of federal forms are not acceptable. In financial aid circles, this form is commonly referred to by its initials: FAFSA. The FAFSA determines your eligibility status for all grants and loans provided by federal or state governments and certain college or institution aid, so it is the first step in the financial aid process, and it should be done as soon as possible.

Many sources of financial aid require students to complete a FAFSA in order to become eligible for other types of financial aid, such as school-based or private aid. If you are computer savvy, you can visit a Web Site where you fill out and submit the FAFSA on-line. You'll need to print out, sign, and send in the release and signature pages. See the *Resources* section at the end of this chapter for the Web address.

The second step of the process is to create a financial aid calendar. You can use any standard calendar—wall, desk, or portable—for this step. The main thing is to write all of the application deadlines for each step of the financial aid process on one calendar, so you can see at a glance what needs to be done when. You can start this calendar by writing in the date you requested your FAFSA. Then mark down when you received it and when you sent the completed form in. Add important dates and deadlines for any other applications you need to complete for school-based or private aid as you progress though the financial aid process. Using and maintaining a calendar will help the whole financial aid process run more smoothly and give you peace of mind that the important dates are written down and are not merely bouncing around in your head.

When Should You Apply?

Apply for financial aid as soon as possible after January 1st of the year in which you want to enroll in school. For example, if you want to begin school in the fall of 1999, then you should apply for financial aid as soon as possible after January 1, 1999. It is easier to complete the FAFSA after you have completed your tax return, so you may want to consider filing your taxes as early as possible as well. Do not sign, date, or send your application before January 1st of the year for which you are seeking aid. If you apply by mail, send your completed application in the envelope that came with the original application. The envelope is already addressed, and using it will make sure your application reaches the correct address.

Many students lose out on thousands of dollars in grants and loans because they file too late. A financial aid administrator from New Jersey says:

> When you fill out the Free Application for Federal Student Aid (FAFSA), you are applying for all aid available, both federal and state, work-study, student loans, etc. The important thing is complying with the deadline date. Those students who do are considered for the Pell Grant, the SEOG (Supplemental Educational Opportunity Grant), and the Perkins Loan, which is the best loan as far as interest goes. Lots of students miss the June 30th deadline, and it can mean losing $2,480 from TAG, about $350 from WPCNJ, and another $1,100 from EOF. Students, usually the ones who need the money most, often ignore the deadlines.

After you mail in your completed FAFSA, your application will be processed in approximately four weeks. Then, you will receive a Student Aid Report (SAR) in the mail. The SAR will report the information from your application and, if there are no questions or problems with your application, your SAR will report your Expected Family Contribution (EFC), the number used to determine your eligibility for federal student aid. Each school you list on the application may also receive your application information if the school is set up to receive the information electronically.

You must reapply for financial aid every year. However, after your first year, you will receive a Student Aid Report (SAR) in the mail before the application deadline. If no corrections need to be made, you can just sign it and send it in.

How to File Your Forms

1. Get an original Federal Application for Federal Student Aid (FAFSA). Remember to pick up an original copy of this form, as photocopies are not acceptable.

2. Fill out the entire FAFSA as completely as possible. Make an appointment with a financial aid counselor if you need help. Read the forms completely, and don't skip any relevant portions.

3. Return the FAFSA before the deadline date. Financial aid counselors warn that many students don't file the forms before the deadline and lose out on available aid. Don't be one of those students!

What is Financial Need?

Financial aid from many of the programs discussed in this chapter is awarded on the basis of financial need (except for unsubsidized Stafford, PLUS, and Consolidation loans, and some scholarships and grants). When you apply for federal student aid by completing the FAFSA, the information you report is used in a formula established by the U. S. Congress. The formula determines your Expected Family Contribution (EFC), an amount you and your family are expected to contribute toward your education. If your EFC is below a certain amount, you'll be eligible for a federal Pell grant, assuming you meet all other eligibility requirements.

There isn't a maximum EFC that defines eligibility for the other financial aid options. Instead, your EFC is used in an equation to determine your financial needs.

> **Cost of Attendance – Expected Family Contribution = Financial Need**

A financial aid administrator calculates your cost of attendance and subtracts the amount you and your family are expected to contribute toward that cost. If there's anything left over, you're considered to have financial need.

Are You Dependent or Independent?

You need to find out if you are considered to be a dependent or an independent student by the federal government. Federal policy uses strict and specific criteria to make this designation, and that criteria applies to all applicants for federal student aid equally. A dependent student is expected to have parental contribution to school expenses, and an independent student is not. The parental contribution depends on the number of parents with earned income, their income and assets, the age of the older parent, the family size, and the number of family members enrolled in post-secondary education. Income is not just the adjusted gross income from the tax return, but also includes nontaxable income such as social security benefits and child support.

You're an independent student if at least one of the following applies to you:

* you are 24 years old
* you're married (even if you're separated)
* you have legal dependents other than a spouse who get more than half of their support from you and will continue to get that support during the award year

- you're an orphan or ward of the court (or were a ward of the court until age 18)
- you're a graduate or professional student
- you're a veteran of the U.S. Armed Forces—formerly engaged in active service in the U.S. Army, Navy, Air Force, Marines, or Coast Guard or as a cadet or midshipman at one of the service academies—released under a condition other than dishonorable. (ROTC students, members of the National Guard, and most reservists are not considered veterans, nor are cadets and midshipmen still enrolled in one of the military service academies.)

If you live with your parents and if they claimed you as a dependent on their last tax return, then your need will be based on your parents' income. You do not qualify for independent status just because your parents have decided to not claim you as an exemption on their tax return (this used to be the case but is no longer) or do not want to provide financial support for your college education.

Students are classified as dependent or independent because federal student aid programs are based on the idea that students (and their parents or spouse, if applicable) have the primary responsibility for paying for their post-secondary, i.e., after high school, education.

What Financial Records Do You Need?

Your financial need for most grants and loans depends on your financial situation. Now that you've determined if you are considered a dependent or independent student, you'll know whose financial records you need to gather for this step of the process. If you are a dependent student, then you must gather not only your own financial records, but those of your parents as well because you must report their income and assets as well as your own when you complete the FAFSA. If you are an independent student, then you need to gather only your own financial records (and those of your spouse if you're married). Gather your tax records from the year previous to when you are applying. For example, if you apply for the fall of 1999, you will use your tax records from 1998.

To help you fill out the FAFSA, gather the following documents:

- U. S. Income Tax Returns (IRS Form 1040, 1040A, or 1040EZ) for the year that just ended and W-2 and 1099 forms
- Records of untaxed income, such as Social Security benefits, AFDC or ADC, child support, welfare, pensions, military subsistence allowances, and veterans benefits

- Current bank statements and mortgage information
- Medical and dental expenses for the past year that weren't covered by health insurance
- Business and/or farm records
- Records of investments such as stocks, bonds, and mutual funds, as well as bank Certificates of Deposit (CDs) and recent statements from money market accounts
- Social Security number(s)

Even if you do not complete your federal income tax return until March or April, you should not wait to file your FAFSA until your tax returns are filed with the IRS. Instead, use estimated income information and submit the FAFSA, as noted below, just as soon as possible after January 1. Be as accurate as possible, but you can correct estimates later.

TYPES OF FINANCIAL AID

There are many types of financial aid available to help with school expenses. Three general categories exist for financial aid:

1. Grants and scholarships—aid that you don't have to pay back
2. Work/Study—aid that you earn by working
3. Loans—aid that you have to pay back

Grants

Grants are an advantageous form of financial aid because they do not need to be paid back. They are normally awarded based on financial need. Here are the two most common forms of grants for undergraduate students:

Federal Pell Grants

Federal Pell grants are based on financial need and are awarded only to under-graduate students who have not yet earned a bachelor's or professional degree. For many students, Pell grants provide a foundation of financial aid to which other aid may be added. Awards for the award year will depend on program funding. The maximum award for the 1996–1997 award year was $2,470. You can receive only one Pell grant in an award year, and you may not receive Pell grant funds for more than one school at a time.

How much you get will depend not only on your Expected Family Contribution (EFC) but on your cost of attendance, whether you're a full-time or part-time student, and whether you attend school for a full academic year or less. You can qualify for a Pell grant even if you are only enrolled part time in a training program. You should also be aware that some private and school-based sources of financial aid will not consider your eligibility if you haven't first applied for a Pell grant.

Federal Supplemental Educational Opportunity Grants (FSEOG)

A Federal Supplemental Educational Opportunity Grant (FSEOG) is for undergraduates with exceptional financial need—that is, students with the lowest Expected Family Contributions (EFCs). It gives priority to students who receive federal Pell grants. An FSEOG is similar to a Pell grant in that it doesn't need to be paid back.

You can receive between $100 and $4,000 a year, depending on when you apply, your level of need, and the funding level of the school you're attending. There's no guarantee every eligible student will be able to receive a FSEOG. Students at each school are paid based on the availability of funds at that school and not all schools participate in this program. To have the best chances of getting this grant, apply as early as you can after January 1st of the year in which you plan to attend school.

Scholarships

Scholarships are often awarded for academic merit or for special characteristics (for example, ethnic heritage, interests, sports, parents' career, college major, geographic location), but some are also based on financial need. The best aspect of scholarships is that you don't have to pay them back! You can obtain scholarships from federal, state, school, and private sources.

To find private sources of aid, spend a few hours in the library looking at scholarship and fellowship books. See the *Resources* section at the end of this chapter to find relevant scholarship book titles. If you're currently employed, check to see if your employer has aid funds available. If you're a dependent student, ask your parents and aunts, uncles, and cousins to check with groups or organizations they belong to for possible aid sources. You never know what type of private aid you might dig up. For example, any of the following groups may know of money that could be yours:

- religious organizations
- fraternal organizations
- clubs, such as the Rotary, Kiwanas, American Legion, or 4H
- athletic clubs
- veterans groups
- ethnic group associations
- unions

If you have already selected the school you will attend, check with a financial aid administrator (FAA) in the financial aid department to find out if you qualify for any school-based scholarships or other aid. More schools are offering merit-based aid for students with a high school GPA of a certain level or with a certain level of SAT scores to attract more students to their school. Also check with the real estate or business department to see if they maintain a bulletin board or other method of posting available scholarships that are specific to real estate programs.

While you are looking for sources of scholarships, continue to enhance your chances of winning a scholarship by participating in extracurricular events and volunteer activities. You should also obtain references from people who know you well and are leaders in the community, so you can submit their names and/or letters with your scholarship applications. Make a list of any awards you've received in the past or other honors that you could list on your scholarship application.

Here are a few samples of real estate scholarships that you might be eligible for.

Appraisal Institute Education Trust Scholarship Fund

The Appraisal Institute Education Trust Scholarship Fund offers scholarships of between $2,000–3,000 to undergraduates who major in real estate, land economics, or real estate appraisal. For more information, contact the Director of Scholarships, Appraisal Institute Education Trust Scholarship Fund, 875 N. Michigan Avenue, Suite #2400, Chicago, IL 60611; the phone number is 312-335-4100.

California Association of REALTORS® Scholarship

The California Association of REALTORS® Scholarship Foundation awards scholarships to undergraduate students studying for a career in real estate. This scholarship is an academic-based scholarship; however, awards will first be given to students who demonstrate financial need. The two award categories are $2,000 awarded to students of four-year colleges/universities, and $1,000 awarded to students of two-year colleges and to seniors enrolled in their last semester of high school. Students must have successfully completed at least 30 units. To apply for this scholarship, contact the California Association of Realtors, 525 S. Virgil Avenue, Los Angeles, CA 90020; the phone number is 213-739-8200.

George M. Booker Collegiate Scholarship for Minorities

Each year, two undergraduates and one graduate student of real estate will receive tuition assistance from the George M. Booker Collegiate Scholarship for Minorities program that is affiliated with the Institute of Real Estate Management (IREM). For more information, contact the IREM Foundation Coordinator, 430 N. Michigan Avenue, Chicago, IL 60611-4090; the phone number is 312-329-6008.

Harwood Memorial Real Estate Scholarship

The Harwood Memorial Real Estate Scholarship awards $500 to undergraduates or graduate students who are enrolled in a program specializing in real estate (full-time enrollment required of senior college and graduate students; part-time enrollment acceptable for junior college students) and who have a minimum 3.2/4.0 grade point average. Students must have completed one or two real estate courses and two semesters of college work and have plans to pursue a career in real estate. To apply for this scholarship, contact the Real Estate Educators Association, 10565 Lee Highway, Fairfax, VA 22030; the phone number is 703-352-6688.

Paul H. Rittle, Sr. Memorial Scholarship

Primary attention is placed on financial need and a demonstrated commitment to a career in real estate management for the Paul H. Rittle Sr. Memorial Scholarship. Awards are made on a course-by-course basis for students taking courses from the Institute of Real Estate Management (IREM). You may receive more than one scholarship, but only one in a given calendar year. The scholarships may reach a maximum of $2,000 for CPM membership qualification courses and $500 for IREM's Accredited Resident Manager (ARM) qualification courses. To apply for this scholarship, contact: IREM Foundation Coordinator, 430 N. Michigan Avenue, Chicago, IL 60611-4090; the phone number is 312-329-6008.

Real Estate Education Association Scholarship

The Real Estate Education Association Scholarship offers a scholarship of $250 to undergraduates who major in real estate. For more information, contact the Scholarship Committee Chairperson, Real Estate Education Association Scholarship, 111 E. Wacker Drive, #200, Chicago, IL 60601; the phone number is 312-372-9800.

Real Estate Endowment Fund Scholarship

The Real Estate Endowment Fund offers scholarships to real estate majors in California of up to $800 per academic year for low income/disadvantaged students. Students must be enrolled at least half-time and have a minimum GPA of 2.0. You can apply for this scholarship by obtaining an application from the Real Estate Department Coordinator or the Financial Aid Office at your community college.

Sam D. Mansfield Memorial Scholarship

The Sam D. Mansfield Memorial Scholarship offers $1,000 to undergraduates majoring in finance, insurance, or real estate. For more information, contact the Executive Secretary, B.O.D./Florida Land and Title Association, 2003 Apalachee Parkway, Tallahassee, FL 32301; the phone number is 904-878-1179.

Southwest University Fenmore Real Estate Competition

This scholarship may only be used at Southwest University in California by undergraduates with a real estate major. For more information, contact the Financial Aid Director, Southwest University, School of Law, 675 S. Westmoreland Avenue, Los Angeles, CA 90052; the phone number is 213-738-6719.

William Stevens Brown Fund

This scholarship may only be used at Florida Atlantic University by undergraduates with a real estate major. For more information, contact Office of the Dean, Florida Atlantic University, College of Business and Public Administration, Boca Raton, FL 33431; the phone number is 305-393-3000.

Work-Study Programs

A variety of work-study programs are available as a form of financial aid. If you already know what school you want to attend, you can find out about its school-based work-study options from the student employment office. Job possibilities may include on- or off-campus jobs, part time or almost full time; in the real estate field or in an unrelated area. Another type of work study program is called the Federal Work-Study program and it can be applied for on the FAFSA.

The Federal Work-Study (FWS) program provides jobs for undergraduate and graduate students *with financial need*, allowing them to earn money to help pay education expenses. The program encourages community service work and provides hands-on experience related to your course of study, when available. The amount of the FWS award depends on when you apply (again, *apply early*), your level of need, and the funds that are available at your particular school.

Your FWS salary will be at least the current federal minimum wage or higher, depending on the type of work you do and the skills required. As an undergraduate, you'll be paid by the hour (a graduate student may receive a salary), and you will receive the money directly from your school at least monthly—you cannot be paid by commission or fee. The awards are not transferable from year to year. Not all schools have work-study in every area of study.

An advantage of working under the FWS program is that your earnings are exempt from FICA taxes if you are enrolled full time and are working less than half time. You will be assigned a job on-campus, in a private non-profit organization, or a public agency that offers a public service. You may provide a community service relating to real estate if your school has such a program. The total hourly wages you earn in each year cannot exceed your total FWS award for that year and you cannot work more than twenty hours per week. Your financial aid administrator (FAA) or the direct employer must consider your class schedule and your academic progress before assigning your job.

If you cannot finance your entire training program through scholarships, grants, or work-study exclusively, the next step is to consider taking out a loan. Be cautious about the amount you borrow, but remember that it may be worth it to borrow money to attend a training program that will enhance your future job prospects.

Obtaining Student Loans

The first step in finding a student loan is to know the basics of loan programs. You need to become familiar with the student loan programs, especially with government loans. You can get a good head start on this process by reading the rest of this chapter. To get more detailed information than appears here, seek guidance from a financial aid administrator or banking institution.

Ask Questions Before You Take Out a Loan

In order to get the facts and clearly understand the loan you're about to take out, ask several questions about it before you sign on the dotted line. Here are a few sample questions you might want to ask, along with tips to help you seek the information you need.

1. *What is the interest rate and how often is the interest capitalized?* Your college's financial aid administrator or a lender may be able to tell you this.

2. *What fees will be charged?* Government loans generally have an origination fee that goes to the federal government to help offset its costs, and a guarantee fee, which goes to a guaranty agency for insuring the loan. Both are deducted from the amount given to you.

3. *Will I have to make any payments while still in school?* Usually you won't, and, depending on the type of loan, the government may even pay the interest for you while you're in school.

4. *What is the grace period—the period after my schooling ends, during which no payment is required?* You need to find out if it is long enough, realistically, for you to find a job and get on your feet. (A six-month grace period is common.)

5. *When will my first payment be due and approximately how much will it be?* You can get a good preview of the repayment process from the answer to this question.

6. *Who exactly will hold my loan?* To whom will I be sending payments? Who should I contact with questions or inform of changes in my situation? Your loan may be sold by the original lender to a secondary market institution. You need to know the contact information for your lender.

7. *Will I have the right to pre-pay the loan, without penalty, at any time?* Some loan programs allow pre-payment with no penalty, but others do not.

8. *Will deferments and forbearances be possible if I am temporarily unable to make payments?* You need to find out how to apply for a deferment or forbearance if you need it.

9. *Will the loan be canceled ("forgiven") if I become totally and permanently disabled, or if I die?* This is always a good option to have on any loan you take out.

Federal Perkins Loans

A federal Perkins loan has the lowest interest rate (approximately 5%) of any loan available for both undergraduate and graduate students and is offered to students with exceptional financial need. You repay your school, who lends the money to you with government funds.

Depending on when you apply, your level of need, and the funding level of the school, you can borrow up to $3,000 for each year of undergraduate study. The total amount you can borrow as an undergraduate is $15,000.

The school pays you directly by check or credits your tuition account. You have nine months after you graduate (provided you were continuously enrolled at least half-time) to begin repayment, with up to 10 years to pay off the entire loan.

Parent Loan for Undergraduate Students (PLUS)

PLUS loans enable parents with good credit histories to borrow money to pay education expenses of a child who is a dependent undergraduate student enrolled at least half time. Your parents must submit the completed forms to your school.

To be eligible, your parents will be required to pass a credit check. If they don't pass the credit check, they might still be able to receive a loan if they can show that extenuating circumstances exist or if someone who is able to pass the credit check agrees to co-sign the loan. Your parents must also meet citizenship requirements.

The yearly limit on a PLUS Loan is equal to your cost of attendance minus any other financial aid you receive. For instance, if your cost of attendance is $6,000 and you receive $4,000 in other financial aid, your parents could borrow up to, but no more than, $2,000. The interest rate varies, but is not to exceed 9% over the life of the loan. Your parents must begin repayment while you're still in school. There is no grace period.

Federal Stafford Loans

Federal Stafford loans are low-interest loans that are given to students who attend school at least half time. The lender of the loans is usually a bank or credit union; however, sometimes a school may be the lender. Stafford Loans are either subsidized or unsubsidized.

+ **Subsidized loans** are awarded on the basis of financial need. You will not be charged any interest before you begin repayment or during authorized periods of deferment. The federal government "subsidizes" the interest during these periods.
+ **Unsubsidized loans** are not awarded on the basis of financial need. You'll be charged interest from the time the loan is disbursed until it is paid in full. If you allow the interest to accumulate, it will be capitalized—that is, the interest will be added to the principal amount of your loan, and addi-

tional interest will be based upon the higher amount. This will increase the amount you have to repay.

If you're a dependent undergraduate student, you can borrow up to:

- $2,625 if you're a first-year student enrolled in a program that is at least a full academic year.
- $3,500 if you've completed your first year of study and the remainder of your program is at least a full academic year.
- $5,500 a year if you've completed two years of study and the remainder of your program is at least a full academic year.

If you're an independent undergraduate student or a dependent student whose parents are unable to get a PLUS Loan, you can borrow up to:

- $6,625 if you're a first-year student enrolled in a program that is at least a full academic year.
- $7,500 if you've completed your first year of study and the remainder of your program is at least a full academic year.

There are many borrowing limit categories to these loans, depending on whether you get an unsubsidized or subsidized loan, which year in school you're enrolled, how long your program of study is, and if you're independent or dependent. You can have both kinds of Stafford loans at the same time, but the total amount of money loaned at any given time cannot exceed $23,000. The interest rate varies, but should not exceed 8.25%. An origination fee for a Stafford loan is approximately 3 or 4 percent of the loan, and the fee will be deducted from each loan disbursement you receive. There is a six-month grace period after graduation before you must start repaying the loan.

Federal Direct Student Loans

You should be aware of federal direct student loans, which are a part of a relatively new program. The loans have basically the same terms as the federal Stafford student loans and the PLUS loans for parents. The main difference is that the U.S. Department of Education is the lender instead of a bank. One advantage to federal direct student loans is that they offer a variety of repayment terms, such as a fixed monthly payment for ten years or a variable monthly payment for up to twenty-five years that is based on a percentage of income. Be aware that not all colleges participate in this loan program.

GUIDELINES FOR MANAGING YOUR LOANS

Before you commit yourself to any loans, be sure to keep in mind that these are loans, not grants or scholarships, so plan ahead and make sure that you don't borrow more than you'll be able to repay. Estimate realistically how much you'll earn when you leave school and remember that you'll have other monthly obligations such as housing, food, and transportation expenses.

Managing Your Loan While in School

Once you have your loan (or loans) and you're attending classes, don't forget about the responsibility of your loan. Keep a file of information on your loan that includes copies of all your loan documents and related correspondence, along with a record of all your payments. Open and read all your mail about your education loan.

Remember also that you are obligated by law to notify both your Financial Aid Administrator (FAA) and the holder or servicer of your loan if there is a change in your:

+ name
+ address
+ enrollment status (dropping to less than half-time means that you'll have to begin payment six months later)
+ anticipated graduation date

Managing Your Loan After You Finish School

After you leave school you must either begin repaying your student loan, or you may get a grace period. For example, if you have a Stafford loan you will be provided with a six-month grace period before your first payment is due; other types of loans have grace periods, as well. And, if you haven't been out in the world of work before, you'll begin your credit history with your loan repayment. If you make payments on time, you'll build up a good credit rating, and credit will be easier for you to get for other things. Get off to a good start, so you don't run the risk of going into default. If you default (or refuse to pay back your loan), any number of the following things could happen to you as a result:

+ have trouble getting any kind of credit in the future
+ no longer qualify for federal or state educational financial aid

- have holds placed on your college records
- have your wages garnished
- have future federal income tax refunds taken
- have your assets seized

To avoid the negative consequences of going into default in your loan, be sure to do the following:

- Open and read all mail you receive about your education loans immediately.
- Make scheduled payments on time. Since interest is calculated daily, delays can be costly.
- Contact your servicer immediately if you can't make payments on time. Your servicer may be able to get you into a graduated or income-sensitive/income contingent repayment plan or work with you to arrange a deferment or forbearance.

There are very few circumstances under which you won't have to repay your loan. If you become permanently and totally disabled, you probably won't have to (providing the disability did not exist prior to your obtaining the aid). Likewise, if you die, if your school closes permanently in the middle of the term, or if you are erroneously certified for aid by the financial aid office. However, if you're simply disappointed in your program of study or don't get the job you wanted after graduation, you are not relieved of your obligation.

How Will You Repay Your Loan?

When it comes time to repay your loan, you will make payments to your original lender, to a secondary market institution to which your lender has sold your loan, or to a loan servicing specialist acting as its agent to collect payments. Be sure to check out your repayment options before borrowing. Lenders are required to offer repayment plans that will make it easier to pay back your loans. Your repayment options may include:

- **Standard repayment:** full principal and interest payments due each month throughout your loan term. You'll pay the least amount of interest using the standard repayment plan, but your monthly payments may seem high when you're just out of school.

- **Graduated repayment:** interest-only or partial-interest monthly payments due early in repayment. Payment amounts increase thereafter. Some lenders offer interest-only or partial-interest repayment options which provide the lowest initial monthly payments available.

- **Income-based repayment:** monthly payments are based on a percentage of your monthly income.

- **Consolidation loan:** allows the borrower to consolidate several types of federal student loans with various repayment schedules into one loan. This loan is designed to help student or parent borrowers to simplify their loan repayments. The interest rate on a consolidation loan may be lower than what you're currently paying on one or more of your loans. The phone number for loan consolidation at the William D. Ford Direct Loan Program is 800-557-7392. Financial administrators recommend that you do not consolidate a Perkins Loan with any other loans since the interest on a Perkins Loan is already the lowest available. Loan consolidation is not available from all lenders.

- **Prepayment:** paying more than is required on your loan each month or in a lump sum is allowed for all federally-sponsored loans at any time during the life of the loan without penalty. Prepayment will reduce the total cost of your loan.

It's quite possible—in fact likely—that while you're still in school your FFELP loan will be sold to a secondary market institution such as Sallie Mae. You'll be notified of the sale by letter, and you need not worry if this happens—your loan terms and conditions will remain exactly the same or they may even improve. Indeed, the sale may give you repayment options and benefits that you would not have had otherwise. Your payments after you finish school, and your requests for information, should be directed to the new loan holder.

If you receive any interest-bearing student loans, you will attend exit counseling after graduation, where the loan lenders will tell you the total amount of debt and work out a payment schedule with you to determine the amount and dates of repayment. Many loans do not become due until at least six to nine months after you graduate, giving you a grace period. For example, you do not have to begin paying on the Perkins Loan until nine months after you graduate. This grace period is to give you time to find a good job and start earning money. However, during this time, you may have to pay the interest on your loan.

If for some reason you remain unemployed when your payments become due, you may receive an unemployment deferment for a certain length of time. For many loans, you will have a maximum repayment period of 10 years (excluding periods of deferment and forbearance).

FREQUENTLY ASKED QUESTIONS

Here are answers to the most commonly asked questions about student financial aid:

1. *I probably don't qualify for aid—should I apply for it anyway?* Yes. Many students and families mistakenly think they don't qualify for aid and fail to apply. The FAFSA form is free—there's no good reason for not applying.

2. *Do I need to be admitted at a particular college or university before I can apply for financial aid?* No. You can apply for financial aid any time after January 1. However, to get the funds, you must be admitted and enrolled in school.

3. *Do I have to reapply for financial aid every year?* Yes, and if your financial circumstances change, you may get either more or less aid. After your first year you will receive a "Renewal Application" which contains pre-printed information from the previous year's FAFSA. Renewal of your aid also depends on your making satisfactory progress toward a degree and achieving a minimum GPA.

4. *Are my parents responsible for my educational loans?* No. You and you alone are responsible, unless they endorse or co-sign your loan. Parents are, however, responsible for the federal PLUS loans.

5. *If I take a leave of absence from school, do I have to start repaying my loans?* Not immediately, but you will after the grace period. Generally, though, if you use your grace period up during your leave, you'll have to begin repayment immediately after graduation, *unless* you apply for an extension of the grace period *before* it's used up.

6. *If I get assistance from another source, should I report it to the student financial aid office?* Yes, definitely. Your aid amount will probably be lowered accordingly, but you'll get into trouble later on if you don't report it.

7. *Where can I get information about federal student financial aid?* Call 1-800-4-FED-AID (1-800-433-3243) or 1-800-730-8913 (if hearing impaired) and ask for a free copy of The Student Guide: Financial Aid from the U.S.

Department of Education. You can also write to the Federal Student Aid Information Center, PO Box 84, Washington, DC 20044.

8. *Are federal work-study earnings taxable?* Yes, you must pay federal and state income tax., although you may be exempt from FICA taxes if you are enrolled full time and work less than 20 hours a week.

9. *Where can I obtain a copy of the FAFSA?* Your guidance counselor should have the forms available. You can also get the FAFSA from the financial aid office at a local college, your local public library, or by calling 1-800-4-FED-AID.

10. *Are photocopies of the FAFSA acceptable?* No. Only the original FAFSA form produced by the U.S. Department of Education is acceptable. Photocopies, reproductions, and faxes are not acceptable.

Financial Aid Checklist

____ Explore financial aid options as soon as possible after you've decided to begin a training program.

____ Complete and mail the FAFSA as soon as possible after January 1st.

____ Complete and mail other applications by the deadlines.

____ Find out what your school requires and what financial aid they offer.

____ Gather loan application information and forms from your college financial aid office. Forward the certified loan application to a participating lender: bank, savings and loan institution, or credit union, if necessary.

____ Carefully read all letters and notices from the school, the federal student aid processor, the need analysis service, and private scholarship organizations. Note whether financial aid will be sent before or after you are notified about admission, and how exactly you will receive the money.

____ Report any changes in your financial resources or expenses to your financial aid office so they can adjust your award accordingly.

____ Re-apply each year.

Financial Aid Acronyms Key

COA	Cost of Attendance
CWS	College Work-Study
EFC	Expected Family Contribution
EFT	Electronic Funds Transfer
ESAR	Electronic Student Aid Report
ETS	Educational Testing Service
FAA	Financial Aid Administrator
FAF	Financial Aid Form
FAFSA	Free Application for Federal Student Aid
FAO	Financial Aid Office
FDSLP	Federal Direct Student Loan Program
FFELP	Federal Family Education Loan Program
FSEOG	Federal Supplemental Educational Opportunity Grant
FWS	Federal Work-Study
GSL	Guaranteed Student Loan
PC	Parent Contribution
PLUS	Parent Loan for Undergraduate Students
SAP	Satisfactory Academic Progress
SC	Student Contribution
SLS	Supplemental Loan for Students

GLOSSARY OF FINANCIAL AID TERMS

Accrued interest: Interest that accumulates on the unpaid principal balance of your loan.

Capitalization of interest: Addition of accrued interest to the principal balance of your loan which increases both your total debt and monthly payments.

Default: Failure to repay your education loan.

Deferment: A period when a borrower, who meets certain criteria, may suspend loan payments.

Delinquency: Failure to make payments when due.

Disbursement: Loan funds issued by the lender.

Forbearance: Temporary adjustment to repayment schedule for cases of financial hardship.

Grace period: Specified period of time after you graduate or leave school during which you need not make payments.

Holder: The institution that currently owns your loan.

In-school grace, and deferment interest subsidy: Interest the federal government pays for borrowers on some loans while the borrower is in school, during authorized deferments, and during grace periods.

Interest: Cost you pay to borrow money.

Interest-only payment: A payment that covers only interest owed on the loan and none of the principal balance.

Lender (Originator): Puts up the money when you take out a loan. Most lenders are financial institutions, but some state agencies and schools make loans too.

Origination fee: Fee, deducted from the principal, that is paid to the federal government to offset its cost of the subsidy to borrowers under certain loan programs.

Principal: Amount you borrow, which may increase as a result of capitalization of interest, and the amount on which you pay interest.

Promissory note: Contract between you and the lender that includes all the terms and conditions under which you promise to repay your loan.

Secondary markets: Institutions that buy student loans from originating lenders, thus providing lenders with funds to make new loans.

Servicer: Organization that administers and collects your loan. May be either the holder of your loan or an agent acting on behalf of the holder.

FINANCIAL AID RESOURCES

Here are several additional resources that you can use to obtain more information about financial aid.

Telephone Numbers

These phone numbers may be of help to you when completing your financial aid application forms:

Federal Student Aid Information Center (U. S. Department of Education)
    Hotline 800-4-FED-AID (800-433-3243)
    TDD Number for Hearing-Impaired 800-730-8913
    For suspicion of fraud or abuse of federal aid....800-MIS-USED (800-647-8733)
Selective Service..847-688-6888
Immigration and Naturalization (INS) 415-705-4205
Internal Revenue Service (IRS) 800-829-1040
Social Security Administration..800-772-1213

National Merit Scholarship Corporation 708-866-5100

Sallie Mae's College AnswerSM Service..800-222-7183

Career College Association 202-336-6828

ACT: American College Testing program...916-361-0656
    (about forms submitted to the need analysis servicer)

College Scholarship Service (CSS) ....609-771-7725; TDD 609-883-7051

Need Access/Need Analysis Service...800-282-1550

FAFSA on the WEB Processing/Software Problems.............................800-801-0576

Web Sites

Check out these Web Sites for information about financial aid:

www.ed.gov/prog_info/SFAStudentGuide
> The *Student Guide* is a free informative brochure about financial aid; it's available online at the Department of Education's Web address listed here.

http://www.ed.gov\prog_info\SFA\FAFSA
> This site offers students help in completing the FAFSA.

http://www.ed.gov/offices/OPE/t4_codes.html
> This site offers a list of Title IV school codes that you may need to complete the FAFSA.

http://www.ed.gov/offices/OPE/express.html
> This site enables you to fill out and submit the FAFSA on-line. You'll need to print out, sign, and send in the release and signature pages.

http://www.finaid.org/finaid
> This is one of the most comprehensive Web Sites for financial aid information. They have many pages addressing special situations, such as international students, bankruptcy, defaulting on student loans, divorced parents, financially unsupportive parents, and myths about financial aid.

http://www.finaid.org/finaid/phone.html
> This site lists telephone numbers specific to loan programs, loan consolidations, tuition payment plans, and state prepaid tuition plans.

http://www.finaid.org/finaid/documents.html

> Free online documents can be found at this site.

http://www.finaid.org/finaid/vendors/software.html

> Software for EFC calculators and financial aid planning and advice are at this site.

http://www.career.org

> This is the Web Site of the Career College Association (CCA). It offers a limited number of scholarships for attendance at private proprietary schools. Contact CCA for further information at 750 First Street, NE, Suite 900, Washington, DC 20002-4242.

http://www.salliemae.com

> Web Site for Sallie Mae that contains information about loan programs.

http://www.fastWeb.com

> This site is called FastWEB. If you answer a few simple questions for them (such as name and address, geographical location, associations and organizations that you are affiliated with, age, and so on), they will give you a free list of possible scholarships you might qualify for. Their database is updated regularly, and your list gets updated when new scholarships are added that fit your profile. FastWEB boasts that more than 20,000 students access their site every day.

Books and Pamphlets

Take a look at the any of the following books and pamphlets to get more information about the financial aid process.

The Student Guide

Published by the U.S. Department of Education, this is *the* handbook about federal aid programs. To get a printed copy, call 1-800-4-FED-AID.

Looking for Student Aid

Published by the U.S. Department of Education, this is an overview of sources of information about financial aid. To get a printed copy, call 1-800-4-FED-AID.

The Best Resources for College Financial Aid 1996/97, by Michael Osborn. Published by Resource Pathways Inc., 1996.

This book lists resources available to students, parents, and counselors—books, Web Sites, CD-ROMs, videos, software—and then recommends the most useful for each stage in the financial aid and scholarship search. It includes a concise description and evaluation of each resource.

10-Minute Guide to Paying for College, by William D. Van Dusen and Bart Astor. Published by Arco Publishing, 1996.

A quick, simple, step-by-step guide for getting through the financial aid process that answers the most pressing financial aid questions. Both parents and students will appreciate this easy-to-use book.

College Financial Aid for Dummies, by Herm Davis and Joyce Kennedy. Published by IDG Books Worldwide, 1997.

This fun and friendly reference guides readers through the financial aid maze by covering the major types of loans, grants, and scholarships available with strategies for how to find and secure them.

Financial Aid Titles Updated Every Year

Annual Register of Grant Support. Chicago: Marquis.

A's and B's of Academic Scholarships. Alexandria, VA: Octameron.

Chronicle Student Aid Annual. Moravia, NY: Chronicle Guidance.

College Blue Book. Scholarships, Fellowships, Grants and Loans. New York: Macmillan.

College Financial Aid Annual. New York: Prentice-Hall.

Don't Miss Out: the Ambitious Student's Guide to Financial Aid. Alexandria, VA: Octameron.

Paying Less for College. Princeton: Peterson's Guides.

Financial Aid Titles Updated Every Two Years

Directory of Financial Aid for Minorities. San Carlos, CA: Reference Service Press.

Directory of Financial Aid for Women. San Carlos, CA: Reference Service Press.

Financial Aid for Higher Education. Dubuque, IA: Wm. C. Brown.

Financial Aid for the Disabled and their Families. San Carlos, CA: Reference Service Press.

*F*ree *A*pplication *for* *F*ederal *S*tudent *A*id
1997–98 School Year

WARNING: If you purposely give false or misleading information on this form, you may be fined $10,000, sent to prison, or both.

"You" and "your" on this form always mean the student who wants aid.

Form Approved
OMB No. 1840-0110
App. Exp. 6/30/98

U.S. Department of Education
Student Financial
Assistance Programs

Use dark ink. Make capital letters and numbers clear and legible. `E X M 2 4`   *Fill in ovals completely. Only one oval per question.* ● Correct   ***Incorrect marks will be ignored.*** ⊗ ✓ Incorrect

---

Section A: You (the student)

1–3. Your name

Your title (optional)

1. Last name   2. First name   3. M.I.

Mr. ○ 1   Miss, Mrs., or Ms. ○ 2

4–7. Your permanent mailing address
(All mail will be sent to this address. See Instructions, page 2 for state/country abbreviations.)

4. Number and street (Include apt. no.)

5. City   6. State   7. ZIP code

8. Your social security number (SSN) *(Don't leave blank. See Instructions, page 2.)*

9. Your date of birth   Month   Day   Year   `1 9`

10. Your permanent home telephone number   Area code

11. Your state of legal residence   State

12. Date you became a legal resident of the state in question 11 *(See Instructions, page 2.)*   Month   Day   Year   `1 9`

13–14. Your driver's license number *(Include the state abbreviation. If you don't have a license, write in "None.")*   State   License number

15–16. Are you a U.S. citizen?
(See Instructions, pages 2–3.)

Yes, I am a U.S. citizen. ○ 1
No, but I am an eligible noncitizen. ○ 2

A `                    `

No, neither of the above. ○ 3

17. As of today, are you married? *(Fill in only one oval.)*

I am not married. (I am single, widowed, or divorced.) ○ 1
I am married. ○ 2
I am separated from my spouse. ○ 3

18. Date you were married, separated, divorced, or widowed. If divorced, use date of divorce or separation, whichever is earlier.
(If never married, leave blank.)   Month   Year   `1 9`

19. Will you have your first bachelor's degree before July 1, 1997?   Yes ○ 1   No ○ 2

Section B: Education Background

20–21. Date that you (the student) received, or will receive, your high school diploma, either—
(Enter one date. Leave blank if the question does not apply to you.)

• by graduating from high school   **20.**   Month   Year   `1 9`

OR

• by earning a GED   **21.**   Month   Year   `1 9`

22–23. Highest educational level or grade level your father and your mother completed. *(Fill in one oval for each parent. See Instructions, page 3.)*

	22. Father	23. Mother
elementary school (K–8)	○ 1	○ 1
high school (9–12)	○ 2	○ 2
college or beyond	○ 3	○ 3
unknown	○ 4	○ 4

If you (and your family) have **unusual circumstances**, complete this form and then check with your financial aid administrator. Examples:

• tuition expenses at an elementary or secondary school,
• unusual medical or dental expenses not covered by insurance,

• a family member who recently became unemployed, or
• other unusual circumstances such as changes in income or assets that might affect your eligibility for student financial aid.

Section C: Your Plans *Answer these questions about your college plans.*

24–28. Your expected enrollment status for the 1997–98 school year

(See Instructions, page 3.)

School term	Full time	3/4 time	1/2 time	Less than 1/2 time	Not enrolled
24. Summer term '97	○ 1	○ 2	○ 3	○ 4	○ 5
25. Fall semester/qtr. '97	○ 1	○ 2	○ 3	○ 4	○ 5
26. Winter quarter '97-98	○ 1	○ 2	○ 3	○ 4	○ 5
27. Spring semester/qtr. '98	○ 1	○ 2	○ 3	○ 4	○ 5
28. Summer term '98	○ 1	○ 2	○ 3	○ 4	○ 5

29. Your course of study *(See Instructions for code, page 3.)* `Code`

30. College degree/certificate you expect to receive *(See Instructions for code, page 3.)*

31. Date you expect to receive your degree/certificate `Month Day Year`

32. Your grade level during the 1997–98 school year *(Fill in only one.)*

1st yr./never attended college	○ 1	5th year/other undergraduate	○ 6
1st yr./attended college before	○ 2	1st year graduate/professional	○ 7
2nd year/sophomore	○ 3	2nd year graduate/professional	○ 8
3rd year/junior	○ 4	3rd year graduate/professional	○ 9
4th year/senior	○ 5	Beyond 3rd year graduate/professional	○ 10

33–35. In addition to grants, what other types of financial aid are you (and your parents) interested in? *(See Instructions, page 3.)*

33. Student employment　Yes ○ 1　No ○ 2

34. Student loans　Yes ○ 1　No ○ 2

35. Parent loans for students　Yes ○ 1　No ○ 2

36. If you are (or were) in college, do you plan to attend **that same college** in 1997–98? *(If this doesn't apply to you, leave blank.)*　Yes ○ 1　No ○ 2

37. For how many dependents will you (the student) pay child care or elder care expenses in 1997–98?

38–39. Veterans education benefits you expect to receive from July 1, 1997 through June 30, 1998

38. Amount per month　$ `    ` .00

39. Number of months

Section D: Student Status

40. Were you born **before** January 1, 1974? .... Yes ○ 1　No ○ 2

41. Are you a veteran of the U.S. Armed Forces? .... Yes ○ 1　No ○ 2

42. Will you be enrolled in a graduate or professional program (beyond a bachelor's degree) in 1997-98? .... Yes ○ 1　No ○ 2

43. Are you married? .... Yes ○ 1　No ○ 2

44. Are you an orphan or a ward of the court, or **were** you a ward of the court until age 18? .... Yes ○ 1　No ○ 2

45. Do you have legal dependents (**other than a spouse**) that fit the definition in Instructions, page 4? .... Yes ○ 1　No ○ 2

If you answered **"Yes"** to **any** question in Section D, go to Section E and fill out **both the GRAY and the WHITE** areas on the rest of this form.

If you answered **"No"** to **every** question in Section D, go to Section E and fill out **both the GREEN and the WHITE** areas on the rest of this form.

Section E: Household Information

Remember:
At least one "Yes" answer in Section D means fill out the **GRAY** and WHITE areas.

All "No" answers in Section D means fill out the **GREEN** and WHITE areas.

STUDENT (& SPOUSE)

46. Number in your household in 1997–98 *(Include yourself and your spouse. Do not include your children and other people unless they meet the definition in Instructions, page 4.)*

47. Number of college students in household in 1997–98 *(Of the number in 46, how many will be in college at least half-time in at least one term in an eligible program? Include yourself. See Instructions, page 4.)*

PARENT(S)

48. Your parent(s)' **current** marital status:

single ○ 1　　separated ○ 3　　widowed ○ 5

married ○ 2　　divorced ○ 4

49. Your parent(s)' state of legal residence `State`

50. Date your parent(s) became legal resident(s) of the state in question 49 *(See Instructions, page 5.)* `Month Day Year` `1 9`

51. Number in your parent(s)' household in 1997–98 *(Include yourself and your parents. Do not include your parents' other children and other people unless they meet the definition in Instructions, page 5.)*

52. Number of college students in household in 1997–98 *(Of the number in 51, how many will be in college at least half-time in at least one term in an eligible program? Include yourself. See Instructions, page 5.)*

Section F: 1996 Income, Earnings, and Benefits ***You must see Instructions, pages 5 and 6, for information about tax forms and tax filing status, especially if you are estimating taxes or filing electronically or by telephone. These instructions will tell you what income and benefits should be reported in this section.*** *Page 3*

SAMPLE

	STUDENT (& SPOUSE) *Everyone must fill out this column.*	PARENT(S)
The following 1996 U.S. income tax figures are from:	**53.** *(Fill in one oval.)*	**65.** *(Fill in one oval.)*
A—a completed 1996 IRS Form 1040A, 1040EZ, or 1040TEL	○ 1	A ○ 1
B—a completed 1996 IRS Form 1040	○ 2	B ○ 2
C—an estimated 1996 IRS Form 1040A, 1040EZ, or 1040TEL	○ 3	C ○ 3
D—an estimated 1996 IRS Form 1040	○ 4	D ○ 4
E—will not file a 1996 U.S. income tax return	*(Skip to question 57.)* ○ 5	E *(Skip to 69.)* ○ 5
TAX FILERS ONLY		
1996 Total number of exemptions (Form 1040–line 6d, or 1040A–line 6d; 1040EZ filers— *see Instructions, page 6.*)	**54.**	**66.**
1996 Adjusted Gross Income (AGI: Form 1040–line 31, 1040A–line 16, or 1040EZ–line 4—*see Instructions, page 6.*)	**55.** $ .00	**67.** $ .00
1996 U.S. income tax **paid** (Form 1040–line 44, 1040A–line 25, or 1040EZ–line 10	**56.** $ .00	**68.** $ .00
1996 Income earned from work	(Student) **57.** $ .00	(Father) **69.** $ .00
1996 Income earned from work	(Spouse) **58.** $ .00	(Mother) **70.** $ .00
1996 Untaxed income and benefits (yearly totals only):		
Earned Income Credit (Form 1040–line 54, Form 1040A–line 29c, or Form 1040EZ–line 8)	**59.** $ .00	**71.** $ .00
Untaxed Social Security Benefits	**60.** $ .00	**72.** $ .00
Aid to Families with Dependent Children (AFDC/ADC)	**61.** $ .00	**73.** $ .00
Child support received for all children	**62.** $ .00	**74.** $ .00
Other untaxed income and benefits from Worksheet #2, page 11	**63.** $ .00	**75.** $ .00
1996 Amount from Line 5, Worksheet #3, page 12 *(See Instructions.)*	**64.** $ .00	**76.** $ .00

Section G: Asset Information **ATTENTION!**

Fill out Worksheet A or Worksheet B in Instructions, page 7. ***If you meet the tax filing and income conditions on Worksheets A and B, you do not have to complete Section G to apply for Federal student aid. Some states and colleges, however, require Section G information for their own aid programs. Check with your financial aid administrator and/or State Agency.***

Age of your older parent **84.**

	STUDENT (& SPOUSE)	PARENT(S)
Cash, savings, and checking accounts	**77.** $ .00	**85.** $ .00
Other real estate and investments value *(Don't include the home.)*	**78.** $ .00	**86.** $ .00
Other real estate and investments debt *(Don't include the home.)*	**79.** $ .00	**87.** $ .00
Business value	**80.** $ .00	**88.** $ .00
Business debt	**81.** $ .00	**89.** $ .00
Investment farm value *(See Instructions, page 8.)* *(Don't include a family farm.)*	**82.** $ .00	**90.** $ .00
Investment farm debt *(See Instructions, page 8.)* *(Don't include a family farm.)*	**83.** $ .00	**91.** $ .00

Section H: Releases and Signatures

92–103. What college(s) do you plan to attend in 1997–98?

(Note: The colleges you list below will have access to your application information. See Instructions, page 8.)

Housing codes	1—on-campus	3—with parent(s)
	2—off-campus	4—with relative(s) other than parent(s)

	Title IV School Code	College Name	College Street Address and City	State	Housing Code
XX.	0 5 4 3 2 1	EXAMPLE UNIVERSITY	14930 NORTH SOMEWHERE BLVD. ANYWHERE CITY	S T	XX. 2
92.					93.
94.					95.
96.					97.
98.					99.
100.					101.
102.					103.

104. The U.S. Department of Education will send information from this form to your state financial aid agency and the state agencies of the colleges listed above so they can consider you for state aid. Answer **"No"** if you **don't** want information released to the state. *(See Instructions, page 9 and "Deadlines for State Student Aid," page 10.)* ....**104.** No ○ 2

105. Males not yet registered for Selective Service (SS): Do you want SS to register you? *(See Instructions, page 9.)* ....**105.** Yes ○ 1

106–107. Read, Sign, and Date Below

All of the information provided by me or any other person on this form is true and complete to the best of my knowledge. I understand that this application is being filed jointly by all signatories. If asked by an authorized official, I agree to give proof of the information that I have given on this form. I realize that this proof may include a copy of my U.S. or state income tax return. I also realize that if I do not give proof when asked, the student may be denied aid.

Statement of Educational Purpose. I certify that I will use any Federal Title IV, HEA funds I receive during the award year covered by this application solely for expenses related to my attendance at the institution of higher education that determined or certified my eligibility for those funds.

Certification Statement on Overpayments and Defaults. I understand that I may not receive any Federal Title IV, HEA funds if I owe an overpayment on any Title IV educational grant or loan or am in default on a Title IV educational loan unless I have made satisfactory arrangements to repay or otherwise resolve the overpayment or default. I also understand that I must notify my school if I do owe an overpayment or am in default.

Everyone whose information is given on this form should sign below. The student (and at least one parent, if parental information is given) must sign below or this form will be returned unprocessed.

106. Signatures *(Sign in the boxes below.)*

1 Student

2 Student's Spouse

3 Father/Stepfather

4 Mother/Stepmother

107. Date completed

Month	Day	Year
		1997 ○
		1998 ○

Section I: Preparer's Use Only

For preparers other than student, spouse, and parent(s). Student, spouse, and parent(s), sign in question 106.

Preparer's name (last, first, MI)

Firm name

Firm or preparer's address (street, city, state, ZIP)

108. Employer identification number (EIN)

OR

109. Preparer's social security number

Certification: All of the information on this form is true and complete to the best of my knowledge.

110. Preparer's signature   Date

School Use Only

D/O ○   Title IV Code

FAA Signature

MDE Use Only
Do not write in this box   Special handle

MAKE SURE THAT YOU HAVE COMPLETED, DATED, AND SIGNED THIS APPLICATION.

Mail the original application (NOT A PHOTOCOPY) to: Federal Student Aid Programs, P.O. Box 4008, Mt. Vernon, IL 62864-8608

Who:	Barbara Mason
What:	Residential Real Estate Sales Agent
Where:	Village Cove Realty
How long:	Six years as a licensed Sales Agent in the Real Estate Field; two years as an Assistant in a real estate office

Insider's Advice

A good way to learn the ins and outs of real estate sales is to first work as an assistant in a real estate office before you get a license to sell real estate. I worked as an assistant for two years in a real estate office, and during that time I gained valuable experience and knowledge. In fact, I attended closings and handled the paperwork for so many sales that I became extremely comfortable handling these types of transactions by the time I became an agent. It can be overwhelming to start out in the real estate business if you have no prior experience. I've seen new agents who look completely confused and unsure of themselves because they didn't know even the basics like looking up houses for sale in the Multiple Listing Service (MLS) computer program. Another benefit I gained from being an assistant was learning about the relocation specialization in residential real estate. My experience working with the chamber of commerce to help relocating people find homes helped me to get off to a great start when I did obtain my license.

Another benefit might be to join up with a partner. If you can find someone who complements your strengths in the field, then you can each contribute to your partnership. This is becoming more popular now than it was a few years ago. I worked with a partner for about 4 years, and it worked out especially well the first couple of years. You have to recognize when you need to branch out on your own though. If you find that you aren't doubling your productivity working as a partnership, then it may be time to go on your own. A big advantage to working with a partner is that you have someone who can pick up the ball and run with it if you are tied up with another client in an intense negotiation deal or if you need some time off for vacation or illness. That way, your deals can still go forward without you. Partners usually split all commissions 50/50 and can normally be arranged on an informal basis within your particular real estate office.

Insider's Take on the Future

I plan to stay in the real estate field for the foreseeable future. It works out well that I can work from home and maintain a flexible schedule, since I have two children and a third one on the way! Although you have to put in a lot of time to obtain listings and generate sales, it does feel great when you help people to close on a home that means the world to them. While I wouldn't necessarily recommend a career in real estate sales for someone who needs a steady income to rely on, for others who have more flexibility and who enjoy interacting with people, it can be a good opportunity. You just need to be honest, be outgoing, and be able to accept rejection and disappointment along with the joys of the job.

CHAPTER | 5

In this chapter, you'll find out how to land your first job after completing your real estate training program. First, you'll get the inside scoop on how to conduct your job search through networking, researching the field, asking questions, and using classified ads and on-line resources. Then, you'll find great tips on how to write your resume and cover letter and how to ace your interviews.

HOW TO LAND YOUR FIRST JOB

Now that you've decided a career in real estate is for you, how do you land a job in this exciting field? And where can you find the best jobs? Well, these are tough questions, so you need to arm yourself with the latest information to succeed in landing the best real estate job for you. The good news is that there will be many jobs available in the real estate field. Salespeople are always in demand, and there is especially strong growth in the commercial and industrial sales areas. Property managers with a college education are also in demand throughout the country. While the opportunities are more measured for appraisers, if you have drive, talent, and resourcefulness, then you can achieve your career goals.

WHO WILL I WORK FOR?

Your first step is to find out more about the real estate, appraisal, and property management companies in your local area. How do you find these companies? One good way to begin your initial search is through a visit to your local public library.

Using Your Public Library to Get Information

Your local public library has a wealth of information available about the real estate industry. You'll also probably be able to find some information on the specific real estate companies in your community. Several books in the reference section will prove useful to you in gathering the information you need. Some directories that are widely available in libraries include the following:

+ Dun & Bradstreet's Million Dollar Directory
+ Standard and Poor's Register of Corporations
+ Directors and Executives
+ Moody's Industrial Manual
+ Thomas' Register of American Manufacturers
+ Ward's Business Directory

You may find additional directories that are organized specifically for job hunters: *The World Almanac National Job Finder's Guide* (published by St. Martin's Press) and the *Job Bank* series (published by Adams Media Corporation) are two examples. Both of these directories are excellent sources of information for job seekers. The *Job Finder's Guide* offers brief job descriptions and on-line resources. The *Job Bank* books are published by geographic region, and they contain profiles of specific companies and provide contact information for major employers in your region sorted by industry. Therefore, you can find the names and addresses of specific employers in the real estate field in your region. Just look up "Real Estate" and go to that section of the book to find local companies that hire real estate professionals.

Articles about particular companies in magazines and newspapers can tell you a great deal about them. You can identify articles about a particular company by looking under its name in periodical or computerized indexes such as those on the list that follows. It's best to stick to the most recent issues since information becomes dated quickly. Indexes to periodicals that you'll find in the library may include:

- Business Periodicals Index
- Reader's Guide to Periodical Literature
- Newspaper Index
- Wall Street Journal Index
- New York Times Index

Using your library's resources is a good way to collect information that will jump-start your job search. Since the majority of people who are in real estate today got their start as a salesperson, this job choice deserves an in-depth look.

WANTED: REAL ESTATE SALES AGENTS

Most real estate offices are continually recruiting new sales agents to join their ranks. Most salespeople are not salaried employees, but independent contractors who are basically considered self-employed. Therefore, the costs to sign on more agents are minimal compared to hiring employees who get full benefits. Also, the turnover of sales agents is quite high in many real estate offices, so desk space becomes available on a regular basis. Brokers, owners, and office managers are often on the lookout for promising new salespeople who can bring hefty commissions into the office. Remember that the broker/owner normally gets a percentage of all commissions that a new salesperson brings into the office, so it's to her advantage to hire good agents.

Of course, not all companies hire on a regular basis, so if you are interested in joining a particular office, you may not get it on your first try. Perhaps after a track record of experience behind you, you might break into that office later in your career. While you may not get hired by your first choice, chances are that you will be able to sign on with another company before too long. If you don't yet know what type of company you'd like to work for, there are ways that you can evaluate real estate offices to make objective comparisons among the various companies. Read on to find out what they are.

You Can Get Hired!

The first step is to get an idea of the different types of real estate offices that are available in your location. Most experts agree that you should capitalize on your knowledge of your local area and join a company close to where you live. If you've lived there for at least a year, you probably know a lot of the ins and outs of the neighborhood and could easily pass that information on to prospective buyers. But even when you narrow the list down to the real estate offices in your neighbor-hood, you may still have several to choose from. Therefore, you'll need to actually visit some real estate companies to get a better feel for which ones you'd be most comfortable working in. Several different types of real estate companies exist. Let's take a closer look at the most common types: national franchises, large indepen-dent firms, and small independent firms.

National Franchises

You have probably heard and seen quite a bit of advertising for national real estate franchises. They focus on building brand-name loyalty and national recognition among the buying and selling public, and then pass along that name recognition to each independently owned and operated real estate company that uses their national name. Franchises are buying up independent firms at a brisk rate all around the country. The franchise owner licenses their name to the franchisee in return for a percentage of that firm's profits. One of the benefits of joining a national franchise real estate company is the training they offer. These companies normally sponsor organized and specific training programs to help new sales agents become successful and to give experienced agents more advanced tips and techniques. A broker/owner from Fort Wayne, Indiana says he decided to go with a franchise because of the training and national recognition they offer:

> I've been in this business a long time, and I've seen many indepen-
> dent companies giving up their independence to join one of the
> several successful national franchises. I guess that was always in the
> back of my mind as I gathered information about my options. I
> know I made the right choice because we are doing great financially
> and my agents are among the most professional in the business. We
> take full advantage of all the training opportunities, and I do believe
> that the training has played a major role in helping our new agents
> to succeed.

Franchised offices tend to be more structured than independent offices, with sales meetings, floor time, and other organized events regularly scheduled. These sched-uled events may encroach on your flexible work day, so you have to determine if you can manage to attend regular office sessions. On the other hand, if you have the flexibility to attend these meetings, you can gain valuable information and motivational help. For instance, one organized event at Coldwell Banker is described by a sales agent from Palm Harbor, Florida:

> Our office would schedule a friendly competition in the office one weekend or weekday evening. The sales agents would all be in the office and we'd order a few pizzas and socialize briefly and then make several "cold calls" to try and set up appointments for new listings. Whoever got a listing that evening from those calls would win the contest. It was a good motivational tool and it made cold calling a little easier since we were all doing it together.

Another benefit to working for a national franchise is that many of your office supplies will either be supplied free of charge, or at greatly reduced rates. The national franchise can buy in bulk, thereby greatly reducing the price on popular items, such as business cards, magnets, signs, and real estate giveaways.

Large Independent Firms

Independent firms may have many branch offices in one state, region, or city. They are not affiliated with a national franchise and are owned by an independent party. You may find that the large independent firms that have several offices in one region are similar to national franchises in their organized structure and advanced training programs. However, a major difference is that each real estate office that is owned by a large independent firm will most likely have an office manager/broker who is not the owner. By comparison, most owners/brokers who manage a franchised office are the office manager of that office. So you face a greater likelihood of an office manager relocating to run a different office or to open his or her own office in a large independent company. On the other hand, a large firm may offer more management opportunities should you wish to advance in your own career to an office manager position.

Another advantage of working for a large independent firm is that you can get a lot of the perks of a national franchise, without having to pay the franchise royalty out of your commissions. For well-publicized firms, you get the benefit of a name that has built up a significant amount of local recognition in your community. For independent companies that have several branch offices, the name recognition factor can prove crucial in a local region.

Small Independent Firms

Small independent firms may have one or two branch offices. Most often, they are one-person offices run by an owner/broker and a handful of sales agents. Other independent firms may have only one office, but it may be a large office with 30-40 sales agents that is well known in its local market. Some independent firms specialize in a particular type of real estate, such as waterfront homes, commercial real estate, or upscale condominiums or other type of property. They may have become experts in their area of specialization and have built up a name for themselves in their community. These can be good firms to work for if you want to learn their area of specialization or if you want to get into their niche market in a local area.

You may have more flexibility in a small independent firm since it probably won't require as many formal sales meetings or other training sessions for its agents. Oftentimes, training will be informal and may consist of a conversation with the broker over a cup of coffee instead of a formal classroom atmosphere. This type of office can be a good bet for someone who wants to work part time or who needs extensive flexibility in his hours and in the demands placed on him by the office. Indeed, more and more independent firms are encouraging part-time sales agents as part-time agents are being forced out of many franchise offices.

Regardless of the type and size of the company you prefer, you need to know how to evaluate each individual office that you visit to see if you'd like to join that firm.

HOW TO EVALUATE A REAL ESTATE OFFICE

As you take a look at several different real estate companies and consider each one as a possible place for you to hang your hat, start your evaluation of the company from the outside and work your way in.

Location

The first question to ask yourself is, where is the company located? You probably don't want to add a long commute into your daily schedule, so start looking at real estate offices located near you. You should also evaluate the location of each specific office based on the amount of public contact it encourages. Is the location in a busy place? Does it have a large sign that is easily seen by people driving by? Are there other stores and offices nearby that may encourage foot traffic to the office? Does the building look attractive, and is it easily spotted from the street?

Inside the Office

As you walk up the sidewalk to the door, how does the landscaping look? Is there any? Can you see through the windows? Is there good lighting on the sidewalk and in the parking lot for evening appointments? As you open the door and walk inside the building, what sight greets you? Is there a waiting room and does it look comfortable? Try to view the area immediately inside the doorway as a prospective client would see it. Is there a friendly atmosphere? Does the office project a professional image? Is it messy? You want to find an office that appeals to prospective clients and customers as well as to yourself. You'll eventually be meeting and greeting your own customers in the waiting area, so you want to make sure it meets your standards.

While a messy office may seem suspect, look a little deeper to find out if there is a reason for it. Perhaps the office is in its peak busy season and all that paperwork falling off the desks is actually proof of how many sales are currently being closed by that office. Take a look at how many desks there are and how they are organized. Will you have any privacy? Are there shared offices that you can use when customers want to speak to you in private? Some people may not feel comfortable discussing their credit histories or income levels with you in the middle of a large room surrounded by hordes of other agents and customers.

What About Advertising?

Collect the printed advertising from several different real estate companies to see how they compare. How is the quality of the ads? What type of paper is the ad printed on—glossy high quality color paper or black-and-white newsprint? How are the ads worded? Do they sound high-pressured in their approach? Do the ads have a professional appearance?

Notice any other types of advertising that the real estate company does, such as billboards, radio and television advertisements, the Internet, or a telephone hotline. Investigate each of these areas to see how much of a presence each real estate company has. If you are seeking a company that specializes in commercial real estate or appraisal, you may not find any printed advertisements aimed at the general public. Instead, you may need to ask around to find out where their advertising appears. Perhaps ads are placed in specific industry publications and marketing brochures are sent to related businesses.

Check Out Their Web Site

If you are interested in working for a particular company, you can use the Internet to find out if that company has a Web Site and if it posts job openings. Most of the national franchises have Web Sites that include information about careers in real estate. You can access a company's Web Site by searching for it with the use of a search engine. Your Internet service provider may offer a search engine as a part of its standard service, or you can visit a search engine once you are on the Internet. Here are a couple:

http://www.yahoo.com

> This Web Site is a very commonly used search engine.

http://www.stpt.com

> Here is a way to find several different search engines from one Web Site.

Job Searching on the Internet

One of the fastest growing resources for job searching is the Internet. Many individual companies of all sizes now have Web Sites that describe their company, its purpose, and its job openings. In addition, the federal government, many state and local governments, and several national job banks have Web Sites with thousands of job listings all over the country. Most libraries and many schools allow free Internet access to their patrons. In fact, the Public Library Association has published its own *Guide to Internet Job Searching*. This book contains an entire section devoted to search techniques for the Internet to help you find the most effective way to find exactly what you are looking for. Not only can you find jobs on the Internet, but you can also find helpful career guidance, including resume and cover letter preparation and interview tips. Following are some useful on-line resources you can use in your job search.

Real Estate Web Sites

http://www.real-jobs.com

> This site, which requires registration, contains real estate jobs and resume profiles, experience and skill descriptions, and salary requirements by area.

http://www.realbank.com

>This real estate site has a resume bank for real estate professionals to find jobs and post resumes and profiles; it includes a searchable employment opportunities section.

http://www.cob.ohio-state.edu/dept/fin/jobs/realest.htm

>This is a Web Site from the Ohio State University, Fisher College of Business/Real Estate page that contains helpful information, including: skill requirements in real estate, key job areas, print resources, Internet resources, salaries, facts, trends, and top property managers in the United States.

Career-Related Web Sites

http:\\www.jobsfed.com

>If you are looking for a government job, check out this Web Site. It lists over 10,000 federal jobs.

http://careermosaic.com

>This Web Site offers lists of job postings and company profiles, and it hosts online job fairs.

http://www.monster.com

>This site posts a large number of job openings and offers resume assistance to its visitors.

http://www.jobbankusa.com

>A major source of job postings and career information.

NETWORKING TO FIND INFORMATION

Networking has become a major job search tactic used by people in all industries. However, networking is especially important in real estate because the field focuses so much on customer and client contact. It's essentially a people business, so you will be networking for several different reasons once you enter the profession. You might as well get some practice in this art before you jump into your career. Networking is essentially talking to people about something in particular. For instance, you can network with other real estate agents to find out if they like the company they work for. Or you can network with your friends and relatives to find out if they know of a great broker in your area who would be an excellent mentor. And once you land a job, you will probably be networking with just about everyone you meet to get new property listings or to find qualified buyers—more about this type of networking in chapter six.

You can build up a network of sales agents who work at the offices you are interested in joining. When you call or visit an office, ask to talk to at least one of the real estate agents in each office. While they are probably very busy, most agents will take a few minutes out of their day to talk to a prospective newcomer. They were new to the business once themselves, so if you are careful not to take up too much of their time, they will probably be glad to give you some information. Here are some typical questions you can ask them about the firm:

- "How do you like the office?"
- "What are the benefits of working here?"
- "What is the office atmosphere like?"
- "What do you think of your broker/office manager?"
- "Where else have you worked, and how does this office compare?"

You can gather a lot of good information in a casual way, just by talking to agents from different companies. Many agents have worked at more than one company, so you can get the "dirt" on other companies when they tell you why they left a particular firm. Take notes on what you hear so you can organize the information and access it later. After you talk to five or six agents, you may start getting the information confused.

Expanding Your Network

If you take a real estate course or seminar, try to meet the other people who are attending the class as well as the instructor and any special speakers who are invited in to speak to you. Strike up conversations and have plenty of business cards available to exchange with others. Don't be bashful about asking for another person's business card—you never know when it will come in handy. You may want to follow-up after exchanging cards with someone by sending a brief note or an e-mail to stay in contact.

Maintaining Your Contacts

It is important to maintain your contacts once you have established them. Try to contact people again within a couple of weeks of meeting them. You can always send a note of thanks, ask a question, or send a piece of information related to your conversation with them. This contact cements your meeting in their minds, so they will remember you more readily when you contact them again in the future. If you haven't communicated with your contacts for a few months, you might send them a note or e-mail about an article you read, or relevant new technology or law to keep your name fresh in their minds.

Organizing Your Contact List

There are many software packages on the market to help you maintain a contact list. You can also maintain such a list manually using business cards in a rolodex or index cards in a box. Either way, try to maintain the following pieces of information about each contact:

- Name
- Address
- E-mail address
- Phone number (work, pager, cellular phone, residence)
- Fax number
- Company name
- Job title
- First meeting – where, when, the topics you discussed
- Last contact – when, why, and how

You may want to include sales agents, brokers, mortgage brokers, attorneys, owners, and other professionals in your contact list along with potential property buyers and sellers, or you may want to maintain a separate list, depending on the size of your list and the way that you maintain it. Networking with other real estate professionals can give you inside information on local trends. You can also find out about what other companies are doing and which brokers are hiring. Additionally, you may get the scoop on which brokers hold the greatest market share in the area of specialization that you want to pursue. Then you can add that brokerage firm to your list of companies with which to seek interviews.

After you've narrowed your list down to three or four real estate companies that you would like to work for, the next hurdle is to gain an interview with the office manager or broker who does the hiring for that office. You can find out who that person is simply by calling the main office and asking whoever answers the phone. Once you know who to contact, call that person up and tell them you're interested in working for them. Ask if there are currently any openings and if so, request an interview. Even if there aren't any openings at that particular office (this will be rare), ask the broker/office manager if you can come in for an information interview. That way, you can gain more information about the company, make a good impression, and find out if you could apply after gaining a certain amount of experience. Before you go on any interviews, however, you'll need to create or update your resume.

WRITING YOUR RESUME

A resume gives prospective employers a written history of your skills, knowledge, and work experience at a glance. Your resume should summarize your employment history and your qualifications for the job you're seeking. While there are many different formats for resumes, all resumes should contain the following information:

- name, address, telephone number (and e-mail address if applicable)
- employment objective—the type of work or specific job you're looking for
- work experience—job title, name and address of employer, and usually the dates of employment (including part time and volunteer)
- description of duties you performed on your previous job(s)
- education, including school name and address, dates of attendance, highest grade completed or type of certification, diploma, or degree awarded
- special skills, knowledge of computer programs, proficiency in foreign languages, and honors or awards
- membership in professional organizations or associations
- professional qualifications or certifications
- either a list of references or a note stating "References available upon request"

How to Organize Your Resume

There are many ways of organizing a resume, but the two most common are:

- the chronological format
- the functional (or skills) format

In the chronological format, you list the dates of your past employment in chronological order. This is a good format for people who have continuous work experience with little or no breaks in between jobs. However, the functional format is good for people who have been absent from the workforce or who have large gaps in employment. In the functional format, you emphasize the skills or qualifications that you have and not the dates of employment.

Choose the format that best highlights your training, experience, and expertise. Take a look at the sample resumes appearing on the next few pages to get ideas. Other examples can be found in publications available through your public library or local bookstore (see Appendix B for a list of books about writing resumes).

The length and variety of your work experience is your best guide to your resume's length, but one page is generally preferred for a standard resume, and never longer than two. When you've finished writing your resume, ask someone you trust to read it and suggest ways to improve it.

RESUME TIPS AND TECHNIQUES

Here are a few additional suggestions for preparing your resume:

- Use standard letter size ivory, cream, or neutral colored paper. Smaller size resumes may get thrown out or lost and larger sized ones will get crumpled edges.
- Include your name, address, and phone number on every page (if longer than one page)
- Emphasize your name by either making it larger than anything else on the page, or by making it bold or italic, or some combination thereof.
- Use a font that is easy to read, such as 12 point Times New Roman.
- Do not use more than three fonts in your resume.
- Prepare several different resumes, emphasizing skills the various companies or organizations you're applying to are seeking.
- Be positive and confident in your resume, but don't lie or embellish heavily.
- Proofread your final draft very carefully. Read it forward and backward. Have your friends with good proofreading skills read it. Even if you have a grammar and spell checker on your computer, you still need to review it. For instance, a spell checker would not catch any of the errors in the following sentence: *Their are two many weighs too make errors that an computer does nut recognize.*
- Use bullet points instead of long sentences.
- Include key words that are important in your industry.

- Don't include personal information on your resume such as your birth date, race, marital status, religion, or height.
- Do not crowd your resume—shorten the margins if you need more space.
- Use action words, such as managed, conducted, developed, or produced.
- Be consistent when using bold, capitalization, underlining, and italics. If one company name is underlined, make sure all are underlined. Check titles and dates too.
- Keep your resume updated. Don't write "9/97 to Present," if you ended your job two months ago. People perceive that as misrepresentation.
- Do not cross out anything or handwrite any comments on your resume.
- Understand and remember everything written on your resume. Be able to back up all statements with specific examples.

What is a Computer Scanned Resume?

Many large companies today are scanning the resumes they receive from job applicants into a massive computer database. Then, whenever they want to find someone for a particular job, they just type in the key words and up pops the most relevant resumes. While you probably won't run into this method of recruiting in a small local independent real estate office, you will be likely to find such a system in place in large property management firms or corporate headquarters of the largest real estate franchises. If you believe that the company you want to work for may employ this technology, then you can get prepared by following these basic guidelines:

- Left-justify the entire document, that is, don't use tabs or indents
- Try to use one of these fonts: Helvetica, Futura, Optima, Universe, Times New Roman, Palatino, New Century Schoolbook, or Courier; 10–14 point (but avoid Times New Roman 10 point)
- Don't condense your type
- Use normal line spacing—don't cram the lines together to get more information on the resume
- Use bold and capital letters for emphasis (not underlining or italics)
- Avoid light type and paper that is too dark
- Don't include any horizontal lines, parentheses, or brackets
- Avoid italics, script, underlining, columns, newsletter layout, and graphics
- Don't include bullet points (you can substitute asterisks if you like)

- Print in crisp black ink on a laser printer—do *not* send a fax or a photocopy
- Use keywords that you think a recruiter might search for, so your resume will be one that is pulled up
- Don't fold your resume—send it in a large envelope

These resumes are sometimes called optically scannable resumes. If you are in doubt as to whether you should provide such a resume, call the human resources manager and ask. Of course, if you are asked to e-mail your resume over the Internet, you can be assured that you should format your resume using the guidelines given above. Be aware that more and more companies are recruiting over the Internet and are using the new technology to store and organize job candidate resumes. It's one more reason to brush up on your computer skills.

When creating a scannable resume, you can use more than one page. The computer can handle two or three, and it won't get bored or irritated at having to slog through the pages, as a human reader might. However, remember to always take regularly formatted resumes to your interviews. Human readers will appreciate the formatting you put into it.

References

Employers interested in hiring you may want speak to people who can accurately describe your work experience and personal qualities—that is, your references. How do you come up with references? Well, the first step is to write down a list of people who you think would act as a good reference—former supervisors, teachers, or other professionals you have interacted with. You want to select the people who know you well and who would heartily recommend you to an employer. But, be aware that it's standard practice not to include any relatives as references. Before you narrow down your list to three people, contact each person to ask their permission for you to list them as a reference.

You can include a list of your references with each resume you give out, or you can simply state at the bottom of the resume that you have references available upon request. If you are responding to an advertisement, read it carefully to see if you are supposed to send references. If the ad does not mention them, you probably don't need to send them with your resume. List your references on a sheet of paper separate from your resume, but remember to include your name, address, and phone number on the top of the list. For each reference that you list, provide the following information:

- name
- address
- telephone number
- job title

You may not need to provide a separate list of references, but it's handy to carry such a list along to job interviews. If you are asked to complete an application, then you can easily fill in the information about each reference. After you perfect your resume, don't forget its favorite companion—a well-crafted cover letter.

Sample Chronological Resume

Jacqueline Dawson

524 Hercules Avenue • Santa Barbara, CA 91123 • 816-459-9836

OBJECTIVE

Real Estate Sales Agent

EXPERIENCE

1996–Present
Aimes Mortgage Company
296 Rosemary Court
Santa Barbara, CA 91125

Administrative assistant to owner
• Ordered, organized, and analyzed credit reports
• Pre-qualified buyers for specific loan programs
• Maintained files and records, did light bookkeeping
• Assisted manager with marketing duties
• Composed and typed correspondence

1994–1996
Glass Block Designs
126 Colorado Boulevard
Pasadena, CA 91054

Sales clerk
• Worked part time while in high school
• Learned basic selling techniques
• Operated cashier machine

EDUCATION

Certificate in Real Estate Principles and Practices (29 credit hours) from El Camino College, Torrance, CA. 1998

Diploma. Valley High School. Pasadena, CA. 1996

QUALIFICATIONS AND SKILLS
• Familiar with Windows 3.1 and Windows 95
• Excellent time-management and organizational skills
• Excellent written and verbal communications skills

Sample Functional Resume

HABIB HUSNI
1916 York Drive
Jersey City, NJ 07306
201-784-2358

OBJECTIVE: Residential Real Estate Appraiser

QUALIFICATIONS
- Three years of experience as residential appraiser
- State Certified as Residential Real Estate Appraiser
- Four years of experience as residential sales agent
- Sound knowledge of appraisal methods, terminology, and techniques
- Extensive knowledge of real estate trends, market, and laws

PROFESSIONAL EXPERIENCE
- Appraised one to four family residences for tax assessment
- Experienced with reviewing HUD-FHA 203(K) Plans
- Wrote manual for training new appraiser trainees
- Experienced in using market data, income, and cost approaches
- Skilled at conducting feasibility studies
- Map and blueprint reading

EMPLOYMENT HISTORY

Real Estate Appraiser, Brynmeiser Associates, Inc., 1997-Present

Real Estate Appraiser Trainee, Kings County Tax Office, 1996-1997

Residential Real Estate Sales Agent with A+ Realty and Realty One, 1992-1996

EDUCATION

B. A. in Business Administration with a concentration in Real Estate from Cornell University in Ithaca, New York, 1989.

65 hours of continuing education credits from the National Association of Real Estate Appraisers and the Appraisal Institute.

Sample Scannable Resume

Chris Nyugen
1450 Ocean View Court
San Diego, CA 94555
415-555-9876

Objective
Property Manager

Keywords
General Manager, Lease Negotiation, Income and Expense Reports, Customer Service, Communicator, Bachelor of Arts, Commercial Real Estate, Investment Properties

Skills
• successful in lease negotiations
• manage sub-contractors
• research land use
• proficient in Microsoft Word for Windows, Excel, Lotus 1-2-3
• experienced in customer relations and service—friendly, professional, personable
• excellent written and verbal communication skills
• self-motivated, independent worker

Professional Highlights
Macy Property Management, Inc.
Assistant Property Manager, 1997-present
San Diego, CA

Duties:
• collect and deposit rental payments for 52 units
• handle lease negotiations
• complete accounts receivable and payable reports
• secure and manage sub-contractors
• respond to tenant complaints

Grove Apartment Village
San Diego, CA
On-Site Residence Manager, 1988-1993

Duties:
• collect and deposit rents for 16 units
• conduct move-out inspections of properties
• perform routine maintenance for tenants
• obtain sub-contractors for major repairs
• maintain income and expense log

Education
Bachelor of Business Administration. Major: Real Estate
University of Georgia, 1997.

WRITING A COVER LETTER

A cover letter is a way to introduce yourself to prospective employers. It should be brief and capture the employer's attention, but it should not repeat too much of what is in the resume. Follow a business letter format, and include the following information in a cover letter:

- the name and address of the specific person to whom the letter is addressed
- the name of the job you are applying for, if known
- the reason for your interest in the company or position
- your main qualifications for the position (in brief)
- a request for an interview
- your phone number and address

A hiring manager may have several job openings at one time, so you should clearly describe which job you are applying for. If you are responding to an advertisement in the newspaper, you can copy the job title directly out of the advertisement. After all, the hiring manager probably wrote the ad and is very familiar with the terminology. Many human resources departments track the success of their ads, so include the source where you saw the position advertised.

Take the time to do some investigating, so you can address your cover letter to someone in particular, if possible. Call the company and ask for the hiring manager's name or the Human Resource representative's name. If it is the company's policy not to give out names, at least get the person's formal title and use that in place of the person's name.

In the body of your cover letter, think of a way to summarize your qualifications effectively. You obviously don't have room to list the details of all the jobs you have held, so try to come up with a powerful summary, such as "I have three years' experience in real estate residential sales and two years' experience in industrial sales." You can draw attention to the most important part of your resume, but don't get bogged down in several referrals. Show enthusiasm for the job in your cover letter and express your desire for obtaining an interview in a clear, straightforward manner.

After you perfect your cover letter and resume, you'll be ready to prepare for the all-important interview.

Sample Cover Letter

Joshua Milinkovich
76 Round Street, Apt. 10
Kansas City, MO 64112
415-762-1234

September 8, 1998

Valerie Williams
Senior Property Manager
1916 Main Street, Suite 304
Kansas City, MO 64110

Dear Ms. Williams:

I am very interested in applying for the position of residential appraiser listed in *The Kansas City Star* on September 7, 1998.

As you can see from my enclosed resume, I worked as a residential appraiser in St. Louis for nine months prior to moving to Kansas City. During that time, I completed the education requirement for my state certification as a residential appraiser. I am experienced using a variety of appraisal methods, particularly the market data and cost approaches. My research skills, attention to detail, and sound judgment make me an excellent candidate for this position.

Should you agree that my qualifications are a good match for your needs, please call me at 762-1234. I look forward to meeting you. Thank you in advance for your time and consideration.

Sincerely,

Joshua Milinkovich

Encl.

ACING YOUR INTERVIEW

During the course of your career, you'll probably go on several job interviews. At some point, you may even be sitting on the other side of the desk, interviewing people for a job in *your* company. So you might as well spend some time getting more familiar with the whole interview process.

What to Do During the Interview

Greet your interviewer with a firm handshake and an enthusiastic smile. This is no time to be shy or timid. Focus on speaking confidently throughout the interview and answer questions in complete sentences, not just *yes* or *no*. However, don't ramble on too long answering any one question. A good rule of thumb is to keep your answers under two to three minutes each. Prepare carefully for each interview—learn as much as you can about the company before you go on the interview. It will help you sound knowledgeable, and it will help you to evaluate the company while you're on the inside. You might want to practice asking and answering questions that might arise in an interview with a friend or family member to brush up on your presentation and communication skills. The following table contains some of the most common interview questions and tips on how to answer them.

Question	Answer Tip
Tell me about yourself.	You don't have to provide any personal information in your answer (marital status, religion, hobbies). Focus on information about your training, qualifications, and work experience. Practice answering this question before you go on an interview; it can be disarming if you're not ready for it.
What are your strengths and weaknesses?	Be honest. They want to know because they are evaluating not only your skills and education but how well you will fit in to the work environment. If you aren't honest, it will show up eventually. Emphasize your strengths more than your weaknesses and mention only weaknesses that won't break the company.
What do you know about our company?	This is the opportunity to impress the hiring manager by showing that you had the initiative and drive to research the company before you interviewed. Make sure you have something positive to say.
Do you have plans for continuing education?	In any real estate specialty, continuing education is looked on favorably. Most states require that you complete continuing education courses to renew your sales license, so be aware of what those requirements are before you go on an interview.
Why did you leave your last job?	No matter how bad the circumstances may have been, always frame your reason in a positive light. You might want to say something like "I wanted more responsibility" or "I wanted more growth opportunities." Don't ever say it was because you hated your boss!

Try to appear relaxed during your interview—the best ways to do this are to get enough sleep the night before and to be prepared when you go in with knowledge about the company and what questions you want to ask. Also, make sure to project a professional appearance by dressing neatly and fairly conservatively. Here are a few more tips on how to ace your interviews:

- arrive early or exactly on time—before the day of the interview, know where the company is located, and give yourself enough time to find the exact office
- learn the name of your interviewer and shake hands when you meet
- during the interview, make eye contact, speak clearly, and maintain good posture
- use standard formal English and avoid slang
- if you're asked about a skill you don't possess, admit it, but say you're willing to learn
- ask questions about the position and the organization—show enthusiasm and genuine interest
- thank the interviewer at the completion of the interview.

While you need to answer questions in an interview clearly and concisely, you also need to ask questions. Asking the right questions can help you to determine if you really want to work for this particular company or organization.

Asking Questions

The interviewer will most likely ask you if you have any questions at some point during the interview. If she doesn't, you'll need to bring it up yourself. You can simply say something like, "I also have a few questions for you to help me get a better sense of the position" and then plunge in. Have a list of questions ready in advance. There are many things that you need to know about the company and the hiring manager to determine if the company is a good fit for you. It's not just a one-way street where they evaluate you—you are also evaluating them. If you don't ask any questions, the hiring manager may think that you aren't interested in the position.

Questions To Ask About a Salaried Job

Here are some questions you can ask each manager that you interview with for a salaried job, whether it's in property management, appraisal, or related area.

1. What would my typical day consist of?
2. What would my level of responsibility be?
3. What are the work hours at this company (8–5, 9–6, hour-long lunch, ½ hour lunch)
4. What is this company's financial condition?
5. What is your management style?
6. What is the possibility for promotion in the next two years?
7. Do you team up trainees with experienced personnel? For how long?
8. What type of administrative support do you offer?
9. What kind of incentives or bonuses are available?
10. What type of training do you provide?

Questions for a Salesperson to Ask

Here are some questions for prospective real estate sales agent to ask each broker or office manager they interview with:

1. *What is this firm's financial condition? How much market share do you hold? What are your prospects for growth?* While you may not get specific percentages in the answers to these types of questions, you should be supplied with at least a general sense of how the company stacks up against its competitors.

2. *What type of management style do you have?* If you desire a hands-on manager who will guide you through every step of the way, you'd better listen carefully to this answer. It may be phrased so that it doesn't appear the broker leaves new hires floundering, even if that is the case. An answer such as "we have a really hands-off management style here" may alert you to this. On the other hand, perhaps you thrive on independence and prefer this style.

3. *How many sales agents and how many departments do you have?* Large firms generally offer a greater variety of training programs and career options. Employers who have 20 or more agents may also have better office facilities and equipment due to a larger operating budget. If you're thinking about getting into commercial or industrial real estate, you may want to start out at a company that has these departments. However, jobs in small companies may offer more variety and a closer working relationship with your broker.

4. *What type of training do you offer?* Find out how long the basic training program lasts and if it includes training on the company's software programs.

5. *How do you handle the company's marketing needs?* You need to find out if there is a specific plan for the company's marketing, or if it's just haphazard. You'll want to pick a company that has a strong marketing strategy that pays off in a successful image and significant public recognition.

6. *What are the key qualities that you seek in new salespeople?* The answer to this question can help you package yourself later in the interview. At the very least, you'll know what qualities to work on if you do get hired by the company.

7. *Do you have listing or sales quotas?* While such quotas may be a motivational tool, you don't want to have too much pressure on you the first year. Find out the penalty for not meeting quotas, if any and consider it carefully. Not all companies have quotas.

8. *What are the average start-up costs for new sales agents?* Find out if the company offers any discounts or free items to new agents: business cards, signs, magnets, office supplies.

9. *Do you provide errors and omissions insurance?* You'll want to find out if the agents pay for it or if the fee is split with the broker.

10. *What is the ratio of commission splits you offer to new agents? Can I achieve a more favorable commission split in the future?* The industry standard is to give new sales agents 50/50 commission split with the sponsoring broker. However, if you bring in a certain amount of money, you should be able to negotiate a higher split. Some companies have an organized system, such as if you bring in $30,000 worth of commissions in a year, then you get to keep 60% of the commission, instead of 50%, and so on up to the maximum level.

Asking the right questions in an interview can give you the facts you need to make a sound decision when all your job offers start rolling in. After every interview, remember to send a thank you note to follow-up on the interview.

Follow-up After the Interview

Send a courtesy letter to thank the interviewer for the opportunity to speak with her or him. Mention the time and date of the original interview and any important points discussed. Discuss important qualifications that you may have omitted in the interview, and reiterate your interest in the job.

Don't get discouraged if a definite offer is not made at the interview. The interviewer will usually communicate with his office staff or interview other applicants before making an offer. Generally, a decision is reached within a few weeks. If you do not hear from an employer within the amount of time suggested during the interview, follow up with a telephone call. Show your commitment to their timetable. However, don't call every day looking for an answer.

In addition to conducting actual job interviews, you can also get helpful job-related information by going on information interviews.

Information Interview

Another type of interview that you can go to is an *information interview*. If a particular company does not have any room to take on a new salesperson, you may want to conduct an information interview either with the broker/office manager or another salesperson. For other real estate positions, seek out people who are in a position you are interested in finding out more about, such as an appraiser or a property manager. These information interviews are a good way to get more information about the industry and a particular company in that industry. You want to make maximum use of the time a person is willing to spend with you, so ask pertinent questions and be concise. Here is a list of questions that you can ask during an information interview:

- What is your typical work day like?
- What things do you find most rewarding about your work?
- What are the toughest problems you encounter in your job?
- Please give me a general description of the work you do.
- What are the frustrations in your work?
- If you could change your job in some way, what would that change be?
- What educational degrees, licenses, or other credentials are required for entry and advancement in your kind of work? Are there any which are preferred or helpful?

- What are the trade/professional groups to which you belong, and which do you find most beneficial in your work? Do any of them assist people who are interested in entry-level positions in your field?
- What abilities, interests, values, and personality characteristics are important for effectiveness and satisfaction in your field?
- How do people usually learn about job openings in your field?
- What types of employers, other than your own, hire people to perform the type of work you do? Do you know of any which offer entry-level training programs or opportunities?
- If you were hiring someone for an entry-level position in your field, what would be the critical factors influencing your choice of one candidate over another?
- Is there anything else you think I would benefit from knowing about this field?

Conducting information interviews will not only make you more knowledgeable about your prospective position, but it will also give you interview experience, which may lessen the anxiety in an actual job interview. An information interview is also an excellent opportunity for you to learn more about how different companies work and to gain a contact that might help you get a job in the future.

EVALUATING SALESPERSON JOB OFFERS

So you've been offered a job. In fact, if you're looking for a job as a real estate salesperson, chances are that you will be offered several jobs. Most likely, the companies that offer you a position will not expect you to accept or reject an offer on the spot. You'll probably have a week or more to make up your mind. Your task is to re-evaluate each company that wants to hire you. Go back to the beginning of this chapter and review the section about evaluating a company. How does each company stack up against the other? Perhaps one will reimburse your tuition, perhaps another one is right next door to your home, perhaps a third one has a great broker who you really clicked with. You should take a look at all your options, review your notes from the interview, and then make a list of the pros and cons for joining each company that wants to hire you. The last step is to look at the lists and choose the company with the most powerful pros and the least important cons. Then presto! You've landed yourself a place to hang your real estate salesperson hat and launch your new career.

Evaluating Salaried Job Offers

There are many issues to consider when assessing the company that wants to hire you. If you are considering salaried job offers from property management or appraisal firms, you'll have several aspects of the job to evaluate. Somehow you have to develop a set of criteria to judge the job offer or offers, whether this is your first job, you're reentering the labor force after a long absence, or you're just planning a change.

Find out about the nature of the work before you make your decision. Will you be spending the bulk of your time with clients? Out in the field conducting research? Sitting at your desk writing reports? Determining in advance exactly what work you will be required to do may be difficult. However, the more you find out about it before accepting or rejecting the job offer, the more likely you are to make the right choice. Based on what you learned about the job during your initial research and during your interview, ask yourself the following questions:

- Were you comfortable with the interviewer or with the supervisor you'll have? This relationship can make or break your success at a new job. Try to find a supervisor who has the same values as you.

- How long do most people who enter this job stay with the company? High turnover can mean dissatisfaction with the nature of the work or something else about the job. You may not be able to find out this information; however, if there's any way you can, by all means do so.

- What are the future opportunities offered by the job? It should offer you the opportunity to learn new skills, to increase your earnings, and to rise to a position of greater authority and responsibility. The person who offers you the job should give you some idea of promotion possibilities within the organization. What is the next step on the career ladder? Is it a step you'd want to take? Employers differ in their policies regarding promotion from within the organization. When opportunities for advancement do arise, will you compete with applicants from outside the company? Perhaps you want to learn enough about several aspects of the organization, so you can go into business yourself after a few years. If that's the case, find out how much interaction you'll have with other departments and if there is room to move around and get involved in other areas, such as marketing and administration.

After you carefully evaluate each job offer and choose the best one for your career goals, you'll be ready to hop on the fast track toward success.

Who:	Frank Cuttitta
What:	Residential Real Estate Sales Agent
Where:	Becker Real Estate Services, Long Island, New York
How long:	Nine months in the real estate field

Insider's Advice

It's important to find an office and a broker who are supportive of new sales agents. Go around and interview in as many different real estate offices as you can. Ask a lot of questions and find out if the broker and other sales agents have a genuine interest in helping you to succeed. It's really to the broker's benefit to help you succeed since he or she will be splitting all your commissions. However, you'll find that not all offices are as supportive as they should be to newcomers. This is especially true if you want to work part time. In my case, I love my full-time job as a teacher, so I work in real estate on a part-time basis. I am very fortunate to have found the Becker Real Estate Services company because the broker and the other sales agents give me a great deal of support, including passing along sales leads.

You'll also have greater success if you choose to work for a company that has a solid reputation; more people will be drawn to it out of name recognition. In my community, people know that our office's motto is "Long Island's Most Trusted Name in Real Estate," so they tend to call us. A couple of sales that I've closed on have been people who called or came into our office. So it makes a difference.

My other main advice is to keep in mind that you won't be seeing any compensation financially until you close your first deal. That could take several months, and in many cases up to 8 or even 9 months. You have to be patient and persevere because these deals take time—more time than you might think. Therefore, it's important to have another income or significant savings to live on your first several months in the real estate field. Remember, you'll also be laying out money in the beginning for things ranging from putting gas in your car to drive prospective buyers to homes to feeding a meter to other fees and expenses that may not be covered by your office, such as business cards or for-sale signs.

Insider's Take on the Future

I found my first real estate job from a classified advertisement in the newspaper. I passed an approved 45-hour training course and a state exam and completed on-the-job training. Then, when I made an offer as a buyer of a home, I interacted with people from an excellent real estate company who impressed me so much that I am now working for that firm! I plan to continue in residential real estate, and this summer I will be working full time in the field. I don't see real estate as taking over my main profession as a teacher, but I am enjoying my experience as an agent and find that I am using many transferable skills. I am also developing new skills, and one day I may branch out into commercial real estate. For now, it works out great working part time in real estate and full time as a teacher. I have an added bonus that my wife is now licensed as a real estate sales agent, so we get to work together—it means a great deal to have an honest and dependable partner!

CHAPTER | 6

This chapter shows how you can succeed once you've landed your job as a real estate professional. You'll find out what qualities are rewarded and how to increase your level of success. Advancement opportunities and career options related to the real estate field are clearly explained.

HOW TO SUCCEED ONCE YOU'VE LANDED THE JOB

You can achieve success in your real estate career in many different ways. After you break into the field and land your first job, the paths open up to include a wealth of advancement options and related careers, from attaining additional certifications, to becoming a manager, or eventually, to owning your own company. Several career paths related to real estate are open to you as well, from land developers to mortgage brokers and more. Read on to find out how you can succeed as a real estate professional and to see what exciting possibilities are available in your future career.

STEPPING STONES TO SUCCESS

When you talk to real estate professionals, you'll find that most of them enjoy their job, so chances are that you will too once you get started. While the job may seem overwhelming when you first start out, you'll get adjusted soon enough. After investing your time, energy, and financial resources to complete your training program, you'll want to arm yourself with as much helpful information as possible to succeed in your first real estate job.

Succeeding in Real Estate Sales

After you land your first job as a real estate sales agent, you will undoubtedly get some type of on-the-job training. In large offices that are a part of a national franchise, the training will probably be extensive and highly organized. In smaller independent offices, your training may consist of teaming up with an experienced sales agent or a broker who will demonstrate common real estate practices as he works. Whatever the form of training that is available to you, be sure to listen carefully to every part of it and take notes if you don't receive hand-outs about the material that is covered. When you are released on your own to dive into the ring, you need to know what to do with the myriad of forms and other paperwork that each deal invariably includes.

Starting Out Success Tips

- **Give Away Your Business Cards**. If your office allows you to purchase business cards through them, do so right away. You should consider the option of getting your photo on the card if it is not cost prohibitive. Start handing out your business cards ASAP to get the ball rolling.

- **Get on the Company Computers.** Practice opening and working with all the computer software that is available in your office. You don't want to wait until you have clients sitting in front of you to discover you don't know how to maneuver the software to fit their particular situation.

- **Broadcast Your Availability.** Tell everyone you know that you are now a real estate sales agent. This includes family, friends, acquaintances, associates, and anyone else you can think of. Even if they won't need your services, they may know of someone who will.

- **Complete Sample Forms.** You will be amazed at how helpful this is when you begin working with buyers and sellers. You can just pull out your file of completed forms highlighted with any pertinent notes and use the sample forms to help you complete the blank forms.

Drawing from Your Network

Many real estate professionals will tell you that you already have a wealth of business prospects before you even begin your selling and listing career. These are the people who you already know. Sometimes this group of people consisting of your family, friends, and acquaintances is called your contact list, your sphere of influence, or your database of prospects. The first thing to do is to think of all these people as prospective buyers or sellers of real estate. Get the word out. Here are some people you can involve in your network:

- friends and relatives
- current or past coworkers or fellow students
- former teachers
- people you've met at meetings, parties, or even at the airport
- people you meet in the supermarket
- the person who cuts your hair
- your children's friends' parents
- other salespeople who approach you to sell something
- secretaries or other professionals at various offices you may visit on personal business
- people who work in related industries who could give you referrals (perhaps you can find out the restaurants they frequent for lunch and try to bump into them)

You can also network with friends and acquaintances of the people you contact to expand your network base outward to the next few levels. You might land a listing from a person who was related to someone who was a friend of your aunt's hairdresser—the connections can be long and varied, so keep pursuing new contacts all the time from each new contact you make. Follow-up with the networking contacts who give you names of people who may be ready to sell or buy a property.

Professional Designations

Another stepping stone to success is to earn a professional designation from a real estate association. For example, the National Association of Realtors has two programs for salespeople who want to earn a professional designation. They are the Graduate Realtors Institute (GRI) and the Certified Residential Specialist (CRS) designations. To earn these designations, you must meet education and experience requirements. Contact either your local board or the National Association of Realtors for more information on how to meet the requirements. To prepare for these designations, you can take courses on topics such as business development, listing strategies, sales strategies, personal & career management, financial skills, marketing, and more.

FITTING INTO THE WORKPLACE CULTURE

The more people in real estate that you talk to, the more you'll find that every office is different. Each one has its own workplace culture. A real estate sales agent working in New York contrasts two different real estate companies:

> The first company that I worked for did not have a friendly and cooperative atmosphere in the office. I found that I began to stay away from the office more and more often. Every time I went into the office and spoke to the other agents, I felt uncomfortable and nervous. Everything was a big competition. The top producing agents acted like they couldn't be bothered with the newcomers and the other new people didn't bond together either because they were competing for the same sales. I knew it was time to move on, so when I found another company that was owned by some friends of my uncle, I jumped at the chance to transfer. I've been there ever since because the atmosphere is totally different. I wanted to work in a "fun" and friendly office, so I am very relieved to have found one.

You'll get a feel for the workplace culture at your office after the first day or two. Stay alert and keep your eyes open to find out how things are run and the level of formality that is the norm. Perhaps you thrive on competition and would enjoy a highly competitive atmosphere. If that's the case and you land in a highly competitive office, you can follow suit and act like the other sales agents and keep all your leads under your hat.

If you find that you're having trouble fitting into your office, don't worry. It may not be a sign that you need to switch offices. It often takes time to adjust to new surroundings. After you work in a new office for awhile and especially after you close your first sale, you may find that people show you more respect.

Learning from Mentors

A mentor is someone you identify as successful and with whom you create an informal teacher-student relationship. Choose your mentor based on what is important to you and on how you define success. Someone can be successful without having achieved certain titles or positions, so keep an open mind when you're looking for a mentor. The purpose of having a mentor is to learn from him or her. Enter into the relationship intending to observe your mentor carefully and ask a lot of questions. The following is a list of things you might be able to learn from a mentor:

- Public interaction skills
- Negotiation skills
- What to expect in the workplace culture
- How to communicate with your broker or office manager
- In-depth knowledge about technology and business practices used by your office
- Helpful tips for balancing your work schedule and personal life
- Advice about what areas of real estate to specialize in
- What conferences/classes/training programs you should attend

How to Find a Mentor

You'll probably need to actively search for a mentor in your real estate office, unless someone informally decides to take you under his or her wing and show you the ropes. A mentor can be anyone from the broker herself to one of your peers. There is no formula for who makes a good mentor; it is not based on title, level of seniority, or years in the field. Instead, the qualities of a good mentor are based on a combination of willingness to be a mentor, level of expertise in a certain area, teaching ability, and attitude.

There are many ways to find a mentor. Here are a couple of techniques you can try for identifying possible mentors in your office:

- Observe people. You can learn a lot about people by watching them. When asked a question, do they take the time to help you find a resolution or do they point you toward someone else who can help you? The one who takes the time to help you resolve your question is the better choice for a mentor. How does the potential mentor resolve problems? In a calm manner? Do problems get resolved? If so, that is probably a good mentor.
- Listen to people who admire your potential mentor. What is it that people admire about him or her? Do the admirable qualities coincide with your values and goals? If you need to improve your negotiation skills, you probably shouldn't consider a mentor who is known as cold and unyielding.

Instead, look for someone who people describe as personable, responsive, and who has strong communication skills.

Keep in mind that other real estate sales agents are working on a commission basis, so they may not feel compelled to spend several hours helping you along and giving you tips. Therefore, you may find that you want to target your sponsoring broker or office manager to become a sort of mentor for you. However, don't rule out other sales agents because they may be willing to help you out too. Indeed, you can offer to buy them lunch or treat them to other perks to balance the scales a bit when they give you help on a deal or two.

Don't feel compelled to stick with your mentor(s) forever since career growth may open up new possibilities to you in new areas of specialization. If that happens, you'll probably want to find additional mentors who can show you the ropes in the new environment. However, any former mentors you can keep as friends may not only help you career-wise, but they can also enrich your life in personal ways.

Interacting with Supervisors

There is a wide-open field of how to best interact with your supervisors. Some real estate offices have an informal atmosphere in which everyone jokes with each other and engages in socializing. Other offices are more formal and you need to be circumspect when addressing your broker or office manager. You'll get a feel for the atmosphere in your office after a few weeks on the job. Until you know for sure what the atmosphere is, you might want to play it safe and assume it's somewhat formal when addressing your peers and the office supervisors.

Interacting with the Public

Public interaction is an important part of the real estate professional's daily routine; indeed, it is often considered to be the single most important aspect of the job. Positive interactions with buyers, sellers, tenants, and banking professionals will greatly increase your job success.

You might want to consider taking some continuing education courses or one-day seminars in communication skills, public relations, customer service, sales, or public speaking to increase your skills in this critical area. If you have a genuine liking for a variety of people, that natural feeling should shine through and help you out of some potentially rough spots. There will inevitably be challenging people and challenging situations that you'll face in your real estate career.

The trick is to anticipate and prepare for these challenges ahead of time. And taking continuing education courses and seminars can help you get prepared.

Another big concern when interacting with the public is the topic of *agency*. You should have covered this topic during your pre-license course(s). However, any additional information that you can find or read about the topic of agency will help you to perform your duties ethically, legally, and professionally. Historically, most sales agents worked as an agent for the seller and buyers were left to fend for themselves. However, nowadays, many buyers may retain what is commonly referred to as a "buyer's agent" to help them find and purchase their home. You know that several rules apply to the actions an agent can and cannot undertake for the person or people she represents. Be alert so that you do not take any actions that could be misconstrued by either party when you are an agent for only one party of an agreement.

Qualities That Are Rewarded

As you progress through your real estate career, knowing what qualities are rewarded will give you an edge. There are several things you can do to increase your educational background, technical skills, and general effectiveness as a real estate professional. Many of the personal qualities that are rewarded in the real estate field follow the rules of common sense and include the following.

Be Honest

Being honest in your dealings with other salespeople, your office manager, your clients, and your customers is of the utmost importance. If you aren't, your license could be revoked and that would be the end of your promising career in real estate.

Get Motivated

Since your success or lack thereof depends entirely upon your own efforts, you need to be highly motivated. Your motivation to succeed will give you the energy you need to place cold calls and drum up new business when things are slow. It is a challenge to stay motivated when you are not getting paid per hour or a straight salary. You need to remember that your hard work will pay off in commission checks if you persevere and continually motivate yourself.

Practice Public Interaction Skills

Since your work revolves around people—sellers, buyers, tenants, mortgage bankers, lawyers, brokers, and so on—you need to have good *people skills*. These include friendliness, openness, kindness, and a genuine interest and liking for all kinds of different people.

Hone Your Listening Skills

Real estate agents need to listen carefully to the needs and desires of their customers, so they can serve those needs and close the sale. Sometimes you need to listen carefully so that you pick up things that are implied but not clearly stated.

Learn from Your Mistakes

Face up to your mistakes and use them to learn the procedures needed for situations that may be similar in the future. For example, after a listing meeting with a seller that you didn't get, make note of what went wrong and why to help you overcome that obstacle in your next listing meeting.

BECOMING COMPUTER SAVVY

The growing use of computers in the real estate field cannot be ignored. While you don't have to become a computer expert and start sprinkling your conversations with terms like *gigabyte, download, universal resource locator,* and *bandwidth,* you will probably need to become familiar with the basics, if you aren't already. Of course, if you are a sales agent or broker, you'll need to be able to navigate around the Multiple Listing Service (MLS) computer program that lists all the homes for sale by you and other agents and brokers. But in addition to this mainstay of the real estate business are some other uses for computers. Read on to explore how you can become technologically savvy using various computer software programs and the Internet to increase your level of success.

Contact Management Software

One of the secrets to success in a people-oriented field like real estate is to keep track of all your contacts. Traditionally, sales agents who wanted to make a list of all their contacts would write down applicable information on index cards and store them in a box in their desk. Or, they used some other method of taking pen in hand and writing down the needed information.

However, nowadays, you have a wealth of computer software that you can use to create, update, and manage your list of contacts. Many contact software programs are called PIMs, Personal Information Managers. These programs can be used to organize your time as well as your contacts. Other software programs called databases are useful in sorting your contact list once you've created it. You can also create a file in a word processing program that has a mail merge feature to create letters, newsletters, postcards, or brochures to send to your contacts on a regular basis without having to type in all those names and addresses each time you want to send out a mailing.

Whatever method you choose, it is definitely to your advantage to learn the basic computer skills necessary to use some type of computer software to manage your list of contacts. Keep in mind that you can always add to your list through the years; indeed, some successful and experienced real estate professionals boast of a contact list that exceeds 2,500 people!

Getting on the Internet to Boost Your Success

If you don't know a bit from a byte, don't lose heart because you can learn to get around on the Internet in just a few hours. Many public libraries offer free Internet training courses to their patrons. Of course, the bookshelves at those same libraries are stuffed with computer books that can give you an overview of the Internet. One particularly helpful book for real estate professionals is *NetSuccess: How Real Estate Agents Use the Internet* by Scott Kersnar (also listed in Appendix B). This book covers not only how to find your way around to other people's sites, it shows you how to set up your own Web Page. While you may think that this step is too extreme for newcomers to the field, it is never too early to start learning about it. And you just might like the Internet more than you think.

Even if you decide not to set up your own Web Page on the Internet right away, there are other ways to use the Internet to help you succeed. You can get marketing ideas by browsing through other agents' sites and find helpful tips and techniques at real estate related Web Sites. Just go to a search engine on the Internet and type in *real estate* to find links to a vast number of Web Sites.

Using E-mail as a Success Step

As the number of people who own home computers grows, and as the number of people who use e-mail at work grows, so does your opportunity to use e-mail as a supplemental communication tool. You can save time by quickly jotting down an answer to a buyer's question or to confirm a meeting with a seller by whisking off a quick e-mail message to them. You'll find that some of your customers, clients, and prospects rely heavily on e-mail and that they check for e-mail messages several times a day. So it can be a convenient way to stay in touch with them. Many e-mail programs allow attachments to be sent along with the e-mail, so you can attach copies of contracts, listings, and newsletters with your e-mail message. Notice if an e-mail address is listed on a business card whenever you receive one.

Remain alert to comments about computers and e-mail in your conversations to gauge how common their usage is becoming to the people you deal with on a daily basis. You may find out that more people are on-line than you realize.

Real Estate Software Programs

Several software companies have developed computer software that is specifically targeted to real estate professionals. You may find that one or more of these types of programs can give your productivity a boost. In fact, many real estate offices already use some of these programs. If you find yourself in an office that doesn't have any software programs, you may want to consider buying some on your own or along with a partner in the business. Here are some examples of the type of software programs you can use to increase your productivity:

Real Estate Forms:
Print blank or completed forms
View a pop-up calendar
Type in multiple clauses on contracts
Link and copy data from one form to another
Use a spell-checker
Employ the strike-out feature for contracts

Sales and Marketing:
Manage your contact list
Match buyers and sellers
Format letters, flyers, and postcards
Get follow-up reminders
Use tracking system for your deals
Release mailings on a predetermined schedule
Create listing and buyer presentations

Property Management:
Use for homes, apartments, office or retail space
Track deposits including key, pet, and so on
Use for multiple ownership of property
Generate reports on payments to owners and vendors, rent roll, and deposit status

Use multiple account check book register

Generate checks in most formats

Whatever position you find yourself in within the real estate field, you'll most likely be able to find some type of computer software to boost your productivity. Becoming adept at working with computer software programs can give you a big jump on the competition and increase your potential for success.

RENEWING YOUR LICENSE

Chances are that you'll need to renew your real estate license at regular intervals throughout your career. Renewal times and requirements vary from state to state, but you can find out how to renew your license from your state's real estate commission or licensing agency (see Appendix A for contact information). Most states require that you complete a certain number of continuing education credits before you can renew your license. Many times you can complete these credits through self-paced correspondence study, so it's not too disruptive of your work schedule. Some states will allow you to count one-day seminars as a portion of your continuing education credits. Here is an example of what one state requires for renewing a salesperson license:

Sample Salesperson License Renewal Requirements

Twenty-four classroom hours of approved continuing education are required every two years to renew a real estate salesperson license.

Of the 24 hours required for renewal, you must obtain three hours credit in each of the following areas:

- The State's Real Estate Law
- The Commissioner's Rules
- Agency Law
- Contract Law
- Fair Housing Issues
- Environmental Issues

The remaining six hours may be in any of these subjects or general real estate courses. No more than three hours of "Self Improvement" classes will be accepted for credit.

Some states will send you a renewal notice through the mail, and you can just fill it out and mail it back along with your proof of meeting the continuing education requirements. If you don't receive a renewal notice in the mail, you may have to renew your license in person at an approved location. Be sure to contact your state licensing board well ahead of your renewal deadline to find out what requirements are needed.

The importance of renewing your license on time cannot be overemphasized because if you forget, you could get into serious trouble. For example, your license could be placed into "Inactive" status. If that is the case, then you must cease all real estate activity for which a license is required. And, if you do perform any real estate business without a license, you could end up facing a severe monetary penalty. You may also be required to give back all the commissions that you earned after your license was expired. Other penalties may include license suspension or revocation. So be sure to stay informed of your license renewal policies, time frames, and procedures.

ADVANCEMENT OPPORTUNITIES

Some real estate sales agents are very satisfied with their job and their office, and they stay with that office for several years as an agent. Others may join a small real estate office and then move on to increasingly larger offices. Still others will work to become brokers and eventually open their own offices. The advancement route that professionals in real estate pursue is quite different from many other professions because it depends more on the results of their work and the additional training they pursue than on winning the favor of someone in a management position.

Advancement opportunities for real estate professionals may depend on any one or more of the following factors:

- Record as a top producer
- Years of experience in the field
- Quantity and quality of professional contacts
- Availability of management positions in office
- Growth of the company
- Education level
- Management skills

You may have all the qualifications, motivation, and skills needed to become an office manager or broker in your local office, but there may not be any openings available. You can either wait for an opening to occur, or you can apply for a job in another real estate office that has an opening. Or if you pass the broker examination and fulfill all other requirements, you could open your own office or run a branch office of the company you're currently working for.

You have to determine what is important to you when considering advancement opportunities, so that your career choices will fit into an overall plan. For instance, you might want to transfer to another real estate office—by getting a new job in a different office, you can, in essence, give yourself a promotion. You can get any one or more of the following added benefits from a move:

- Higher commission split or lower administrative fees
- Better training programs
- Better office environment, administrative support, and computer equipment
- Better comaraderie with other salespeople and supervisors
- Better reputation of real estate company's name
- More homes to list and sell, resulting in higher commissions (when relocating to a growing area of the country, such as Florida, Arizona, or Nevada to name a few)

Of course, if you land your first job in a solid real estate office that has a professional and congenial atmosphere, lots of training programs, and a solid reputation, then you're all set. You can focus on learning all you can and applying yourself for future opportunities or career challenges in related areas.

Entering Management

You can climb the ladder to success in real estate by entering management in a large real estate firm. Some of the national franchises as well as the larger independent companies employ many real estate administrators and executives in their headquarters and branch offices. Examples of such positions include manager of a particular specialization in real estate, such as relocation, corporate accounts, advertising, historic homes, commercial properties, foreclosures, and so on, and divisional or regional vice presidents, all the way up to senior vice president.

The best way to break into these management positions is to gain experience and education in the area of real estate that you are most interested in and that appears to be growing. Most executives in real estate have a college degree in business, finance, accounting, or real estate. Indeed some hold advanced degrees including the popular MBA degree (master of business administration). However, experienced and savvy professionals who do not have a college degree have also been able to secure high-paying and highly visible executive jobs based on their successful track record in the business.

If you land a job in a large real estate corporation, you may be able to work your way up the career ladder through several promotions in-house. If you don't see such opportunities available in your current company, there's always the option of giving yourself a promotion by seeking a management position in another, larger company. Some management experience or training is usually necessary to land such positions, however, so if you don't possess this background, you may want to consider enrolling in a college degree program or other professional courses. See chapters two and three for more information about real estate schools and training programs.

Advancing to Become a Real Estate Broker

If you decide you want to become a real estate broker, you can begin to prepare right away. The first step is to contact your state's real estate commission or licensing body to find out what the exact requirements are to become a broker. These requirements vary from state to state. They generally include some form of the following:

- ◆ Coursework in an approved real estate training program
- ◆ Certain amount of experience as a sales agent (may range from 0 to 2 years). Significant education may be substituted for this requirement in many states, such as a bachelor's degree in real estate
- ◆ Passing a state licensing exam
- ◆ Getting fingerprinted and passing a background check
- ◆ Becoming a resident in the location you want to become a broker

You may find out that you prefer to be an associate broker who works under the auspices of a senior broker and continue to focus on selling real estate. Or you may want to open your own real estate office and hire sales agents to work for you. This option can take significant start-up costs and it may take quite awhile to realize a profit. Taking some entrepreneurial courses at a local college or university can prove invaluable when deciding whether or not to go this route. You have to weigh the possible benefits against the possible negative outcomes very carefully, as well as examine your own financial standing and ability to get financing for such a venture, before diving in to the process.

Succeeding as a Real Estate Broker/Office Manager/Owner

Gaining management experience and skills will help you to succeed as a sponsoring broker who manages or owns a real estate office. Several options are available for gaining additional management skills. You can take courses at your local community college, enroll in a distance learning program to earn a bachelor's degree, or join a professional organization and take their self-study courses.

One of the many ways you can achieve greater success as a broker is to obtain a professional designation. Here's an example of one:

Professional Designation

The National Association of Realtors offers courses leading to the Certified Residential Broker (CRB) designation. First, you must enroll as a CRB candidate. You must be a member of the National Association of Realtors® and have a minimum of two consecutive years of real estate brokerage management experience. You can take courses on topics such as managing a real estate business successfully, using management information systems effectively, managing people for maximum productivity, interactive decision making, and so on.

Succeeding as a Real Estate Appraiser

One of the keys for succeeding as a real estate appraiser is to become state licensed and certified (see chapter two for more information about appraisal licensing and certification). This will open up additional avenues to you, and you will be able to appraise properties that are a part of federally related transactions. Another key to success is to earn one or more professional designations in the field of real estate appraisal. Here are several professional associations that you can contact to get more information about professional designations and continuing education:

- The Appraisal Institute
- American Society of Appraisers
- American Society of Farm Managers and Rural Appraisers
- International Association of Assessing Officers
- International Right of Way Association
- National Association of Independent Fee Appraisers

See Appendix A for contact information for these associations. Here's a look at two sample designations.

Sample Professional Designations

The Appraisal Institute confers one general appraisal designation, the Member of Appraisal Institute (MAI), and one residential appraisal designation, the Senior Residential Appraiser (SRA). These professionals must adhere to a strictly enforced code of professional ethics and standards of professional appraisal practice.

MAI Educational Requirements

The basic level MAI must complete a certain number of courses in appraisal principles and procedures, basic income capitalization, general applications, and standards of professional practice. To achieve level two of the designation, you must complete additional courses, such as standards of professional practice, advanced income capitalization, highest and best use, market analysis, advanced sales comparison and cost approaches, report writing, valuation analysis, and advanced applications.

SRA Educational Requirements

The basic level SRA must complete courses such as appraisal principles and procedures, residential case study, and standards of professional practice. The second level requires additional real estate courses.

Another professional association that offers an appraisal designation is the American Society of Appraisers. Every designated appraiser must start his or her ASA membership as a candidate member. With additional experience and qualifications, you can become an accredited member and then an accredited senior appraiser. Requirements for becoming a candidate member include being approved by your local chapter, passing the ASA's ethics exam, and passing an exam on the Uniform Standards of Professional Appraisal Practice (USPAP) within a specified period of time. The accredited member and senior appraiser require additional experience and education.

Succeeding as a Property Manager

One of the ways you can increase your marketability and chances for a top job as a professional property manager is to earn professional designations or certifications from professional associations. Here are some of the associations that offer continuing education or professional designations to property managers:

- ◆ Institute of Real Estate Management
- ◆ Building Owners and Managers Association International
- ◆ Community Associations Institute
- ◆ National Apartment Association
- ◆ National Association of Residential Property Managers
- ◆ National Association of Home Builders

See Appendix A for contact information for these associations. Here's a look at a couple of sample designations.

Sample Professional Designations

The National Association of Residential Property Managers offers the Professional Property Manager (PPM) and Master Property Manager (MPM) professional designations. To earn the PPM designation, you must get a real estate agent license, have hands-on experience in the management of residential property, and complete property management courses given by the association on topics such as maintenance, marketing, operations, tenancy, and technology. After you obtain the PPM designation, you can fulfill additional requirements to obtain the MPM designation.

The Institute of Real Estate Management also offers professional designations to property and asset managers. To earn the Certified Property Manager (CPM) designation, you need to demonstrate a certain amount of property management experience and complete several real estate related courses. They also offer the Accredited Residential Manager (ARM) designation for professionals who specialize in managing residential properties.

Other professional designations may have similar requirements. Check with each professional association to find out what benefits they offer their members and read all membership application materials carefully before joining any association.

RELATED CAREER OPTIONS

Real estate is a wide-open and expanding field that offers numerous career choices, whatever your basic interests and abilities may be. In general, training and experience as a residential sales agent offers a good, basic background for other real estate careers. Certain career paths involve returning to college or even graduate school for more in-depth study of subjects, such as finance and insurance, only touched on by the basic real estate pre-license course(s). There are also entry-level career paths in jobs closely related to the real estate field, such as title researcher and mortgage broker that have specific education or certification requirements, but don't necessarily require real estate sales training.

To get a better idea of what could be in store for you in your future real estate career, take a look at the following job descriptions of key career opportunities that are either a specialization in the real estate field or are in a closely related field.

Mortgage Broker/Mortgage Banker

Mortgage brokers and bankers provide an essential service to real estate buyers. Without the help of these financing specialists, many deals would not go through. Therefore, this field is an integral part of the real estate field. Mortgage brokers and bankers help to match up potential buyers with lenders who will give those buyers a satisfactory mortgage. The distinction between mortgage brokers and bankers is this:

> **Mortgage bankers** not only help buyers to get a loan, they also service that loan. That is, they collect the monthly payments from the buyers, and make sure that appropriate taxes and insurance fees are paid, and that the property is suitably maintained.
>
> **Mortgage brokers** do not get involved in servicing the loans that they help borrowers to obtain. Their primary objective is to match up real estate buyers with lenders and get those loans closed.

Most mortgage bankers and brokers not only bring borrowers and lenders together, they also help the buyers through each step of the loan process. This may include helping the borrowers fill out complex loan application forms and giving them updated information about each step of the loan application process. They also often will coordinate getting the property appraised or inspected as required by the lender and making sure all legal requirements are met by both sides of all loan transactions.

Mortgage brokers and bankers work with several different lending institutions to ensure that they obtain the best loan possible for each buyer that they work with. They may work with anywhere from four to thirteen different lenders at any one given time. They need to be very familiar with each lender's financing terms and related costs. Many areas of specialization exist in larger mortgage brokerage firms due to the breadth and depth of knowledge needed in this field. Some areas of specialization include:

- Loan Solicitors
- Loan Underwriters
- Loan Processors
- Office Managers
- Mortgage Sellers
- Commercial Mortgage Specialists

The careers of mortgage brokers and bankers are relatively new in the real estate field; indeed, they have grown significantly over the last decade.

Real Estate Developer

Real estate developers face the challenge of turning empty land or decaying buildings into thriving, profitable residential or commercial developments. They spend a considerable amount of time and money conducting research on site selection. They must thoroughly understand the site, the site's potential, the site's surrounding neighborhood, and the future possibilities for the neighboring land. After selecting an appropriate site for development, developers then analyze the projected costs and work on getting the project financed. After securing adequate financing, they hire contractors and oversee them as they construct the buildings on the site. Once the buildings are finished, the developers oversee the management, marketing, or sale of the final property. It is a complex business full of risks and challenges that could scare off many prospective developers from entering the field. However, along with the major risks involved in land development are major rewards that are realized when projects are completed.

Real Estate Instructor

Real estate agents or brokers who are interested in learning and teaching may wish to become instructors at a private school, a nearby college or university, or other real estate training school. Instructors provide training to all levels of real estate agents, from new recruits to agents who need to fulfill continuing education requirements. In addition to performing as instructors in a classroom, they may also organize or update training programs for specific groups of people. For example, a real estate office may want to contract out to an instructor a particular seminar on a hot topic, such as buyer agency. You then might be asked to come in-house to conduct a seminar on the topic.

Title Searcher

Title searchers play an important role in real estate transactions. They conduct searches to find legal instruments pertaining to property titles, such as mortgages, assessments, and deeds. They read the documents they find during their search and compare legal descriptions of the property in question. They often verify deeds of ownership and descriptions of property boundaries. They communicate often with various offices and agencies, including county surveyors, real estate agents, courthouse staff, lenders, buyers, sellers, and others to obtain the information necessary in their search. Title searchers may also examine individual titles and write reports showing any restrictions to the title along with giving information about how the restrictions may be removed. They need to be detail-oriented with strong research and communication skills.

Real Estate Syndication Professional

Real estate syndication professionals are involved in the investment world. They bring people together to invest in properties as a group. Due to the investment portion of their jobs, syndication professionals need to have extensive experience and education in finance. Many syndication professionals enter the field through real estate sales or property management. They need to have strong communication and persuasion skills when addressing groups of people to invest in partnerships that they have set up. A strong background in general business skills and investing would prove helpful for this career.

Real Estate Auctioneer

If you enjoy the high energy atmosphere in an auction house, you might want to explore the career of real estate auctioneer. These real estate professionals conduct auctions to sell real estate ranging from single family homes to shopping centers. It can be challenging to land a job in this exciting area of real estate, but you can gain more information about auctioning by attending an auction school or talking to auctioneers in your local area. The job has increased in popularity within the past several years due to the need for selling foreclosure properties. Many real estate auctioneers own their own companies, and others work for large auction houses either as employees or as independent contractors. Many of the properties that are sold at auctions come from government agencies and are considered *distressed properties* (ones that may not sell in the traditional method).

SAMPLE JOB POSTINGS

These sample job postings can give you an idea of what type of requirements and pay level are available when seeking new challenges in the real estate or related fields. Of course, job duties, commissions, and salaries vary considerably, but these sample postings culled from a variety of sources can give you an idea of the possibilities that are out there.

Position:	Assistant Real Estate Developer
Location:	Dallas, Texas
Requirements:	Qualified candidates must possess three years experience as a full-time real estate salesperson.
Salary:	$34,137–$47,912 dependent upon qualifications and experience.

Position:	Leasing Consultant
Location:	Fairfax, Virginia
Requirements:	Requires prior leasing/sales experience preferably in the field of property management. Individual must be highly organized, personable, detail-oriented and have the ability to work in the fast-paced environment of a 490 unit luxury apartment community.
Salary:	Excellent salary and benefits package.

Position:	Real Estate Development Project Manager
Location:	Santa Barbara, California
Requirements:	Bachelor's degree required; MBA with concentration in Real Estate preferred. Minimum 7 years experience in project management required (preferably in California).
Description:	Manage all aspect of major urban commercial real estate developments including supervision of architectural design, zoning, approvals processes, leasing, construction, and loan administration. Strong interpersonal, communication, and quantitative skills required.
Salary:	Salary commensurate with experience.

Position:	Title/Escrow Closer
Location:	Minneapolis, Minnesota
Requirements:	Qualified candidate must have three years of experience closing for major accounts. A bachelor's degree is strongly preferred. Must possess strong organizational and communication skills.
Salary:	$28,000-$32,000 dependent upon qualifications and experience.

ACHIEVING SUCCESS

After you close your first sale as a real estate sales agent, complete your first property appraisal, or manage your first property, you will be well on your way to a gratifying and rewarding career. Whether you decide to stay in your first real estate job or move into a related area within the real estate field, you can be proud to be a part of a necessary and important profession. If you pursue each step of your real estate career with diligence, perseverance, and commitment to excellence, you will be able to achieve great success in your career.

Who:	Carl B. Morgan, C.R.E.M., C.R.A.
What:	Senior Real Estate Appraiser
Where:	Brooklyn, New York
How long:	Over 15 years in the real estate field

Insider's Advice

I encourage more people to enter the field of real estate appraisal. It is a career in which you get to keep learning new things every day. Many real estate sales agents and brokers need to have at least some appraisal skills to close the deal when they are trying to get a seller to list their property with them. However, you don't need to become a real estate salesperson or broker in order to break into the field of real estate appraisal. As long as you meet the requirements in your state for getting a real estate appraisal license, you can succeed in this exciting career. Each state's requirements differ, but usually include taking some basic appraisal courses, getting a certain amount of practical experience, and passing the state appraisal exam.

Becoming a real estate appraiser offers you flexibility, since you can work for an employer or you can work for yourself. Indeed, many real estate appraisers are self-employed—they are normally called *independent fee appraisers*. You would probably want to work for a company first to gain experience and contacts before branching out on your own. Personal traits that would help you in real estate appraisal are *attention to details*, especially when conducting research, *patience*, especially when you are waiting for information to come through that you have requested, and *ability to cultivate working relationships* with others, especially those who work in governmental agencies or other firms who can help you.

Insider's Take on the Future

There will always be a demand for real estate appraisers because they provide an essential service. The demand for new appraisers also exists because many young people don't want to enter a field that may not financially reward them immediately. It requires patience to take the time to build up your skills, knowledge, and experience to the point where you are getting significant income. However, appraisers can do quite well if they persevere. This is especially true for appraisers who specialize in a particular type of property appraisal and build a solid reputation in that area. Some areas of specialization are hotel/motel, shopping centers, airports, condominiums, single family homes, and historic properties.

APPENDIX A

This appendix contains a list of local and national professional associations and accrediting agencies that you can contact to obtain information related to employment or training as a real estate professional. Also included are higher education departments in each state—you can contact them for information on local financial aid programs.

PROFESSIONAL ASSOCIATIONS

Contact any of the following professional associations to find out more information about the real estate field. Internet addresses and fax numbers are included where available.

American Industrial Real Estate Association
700 S. Flower, Suite #600
Los Angeles, CA 90017
213-687-8777

American Institute of Certified Planners
1776 Massachusetts Ave., N. W., Suite 400
Washington, DC 20036
202-872-0611 / 202-872-0643

American Land Title Association
1828 L Street N. W., Suite 705
Washington, DC 20036
202-296-3671
FAX: 202-223-5843

American Planning Association
122 S. Michigan Avenue, Suite 1600
Chicago, IL 60603-6107
312-431-9100
FAX: 312-431-9985

American Society of Appraisers
P. O. Box 17265
Washington, DC 20041
703-478-2228

American Society of Asset Managers
303 W. Cypress Street
P. O. Box 12528
San Antonio, TX 78212
210-225-2897 / 800-486-3676
FAX: 210-225-8450

American Society of Farm Managers and Rural Appraisers
950 S. Cherry Street, Suite 106
Denver, CO 80222
303-758-3513

Appraisal Institute
875 N. Michigan Avenue, Suite 2400
Chicago, IL 60611-1980
312-335-4100
FAX: 312-335-4488

Building Owners and Managers Association International
1201 New York Avenue, N. W., Suite 300
Washington, DC 20005
202-408-2662

Commercial Investment Real Estate Institute
430 N. Michigan
Chicago, IL 60611
800-621-7027

Community Associations Institute
1630 Duke Street
Alexandria, VA 22314
703-548-8600
http://www.caionline.org

Employee Relocation Council
1720 N Street N. W.
Washington, DC 20036
202-857-0857 / 202-467-4012

Hotel and Motel Brokers of America
10220 N. Executive Hills Blvd., Suite 610
Kansas City, MO 64153
816-891-7070 / 800-821-5191
FAX: 816-891-7071

Institute of Real Estate Management
430 N. Michigan Avenue
Chicago, IL 60611-4090
312-329-6000 / 800-837-0706
FAX: 312-661-0217
http://www.irem.org

International Association of Assessing Officers
1313 East 60th Street
Chicago, IL 60637
312-947-2069

International Real Estate Institute
8383 East Evans Road
Scottsdale, AZ 85260
602-998-8267
FAX: 602-998-8022

International Right of Way Association
13650 South Gramercy Place, Suite 100
Gardena, CA 90249
310-538-0233

Mortgage Bankers Association of America
1125 15th Street N. W.
Washington, DC 20005
202-861-6500 / 202-861-0736

NACORE International
(formerly International Association of Corporate Real Estate Executives)
440 Columbia Drive, Suite 100
West Palm Beach, FL 33409
407-683-8111 / 800-726-8111
FAX: 407-697-4853
http://www.nacore.org

National Apartment Association
Education Department
201 N. Union Street, Suite 200
Alexandria, VA 22314
703-518-6141
FAX: 703-518-6191

National Association of Home Builders
1201 15th Street N. W.
Washington, DC 20005
202-822-0200
http://www.nahb.com/multi.html

National Association of Independent Fee Appraisers
7501 Murdoch Avenue
St. Louis, MO 63119
314-781-6688

National Association of Master Appraisers
303 W. Cypress Street
San Antonio, TX 78212-0617
210-271-0781 / 800-229-6262

National Association of Mortgage Brokers
8201 Greenshore Drive #300
McLean, VA 22102
703-610-9009

National Association of Real Estate Appraisers
8383 East Evans Road
Scottsdale, AZ 85260
602-948-8000
FAX: 602-998-8022
http://iami.org/narea.html

National Association of Real Estate Brokers
1629 K Street, N. W., Suite 602
Washington, DC 20006
202-785-4477
FAX: 202-785-1244

National Association of Real Estate Buyer Brokers
1070 6th Avenue, Suite 307
Blemont, CA 94002
415-591-5446
FAX: 415-592-2688

National Association of Realtors
430 N. Michigan Avenue
Chicago, IL 60611
312-329-8200
FAX: 312-329-8576

National Association of Residential Property Managers
P. O. Box 10249
Scottsdale, AZ 85271-0249
312-782-5252 / 800-782-3452
FAX: 312-236-1140

National Property Management Association
380 Main Street, Suite 290
Dunedin, FL 34698
813-736-3788
FAX: 813-736-6707

Property Management Association
7900 Wisconsin Avenue, Suite 204
Bethesda, MD 20814
301-651-9200
FAX: 301-907-9326

Real Estate Brokerage Managers Council
430 N. Michigan Avenue
Chicago, IL 60611-4092
312-321-4400
FAX: 312-329-8882

Real Estate Educators Association
11 S. LaSalle Street, Suite 1400
Chicago, IL 60603-1210
312-201-0101
FAX: 312-201-0214

Real Estate Law Institute
303 W. Cypress
P. O. Box 12528
San Antonio, TX 78212
210-225-2897

Realtors Land Institute
(formerly Farm and Land Institute)
430 N. Michigan Avenue
Chicago, IL 60611
312-329-8440 / 800-441-LAND

Society of Industrial and Office Realtors
700 11th Street, N. W., Suite 510
Washington, DC 20001-4511
202-737-1150
FAX: 202-737-8796

Urban Land Institute
1025 Thomas Jefferson Street N.W., Suite 500 West
Washington, DC 20007-5201
202-624-7000 / 800-321-5011
FAX: 202-624-7140

Women's Council of Realtors
430 N. Michigan Avenue
Chicago, IL 60611
312-329-8483
FAX: 312-329-3290

STATE REAL ESTATE COMMISSIONS OR LICENSE LAW OFFICIALS

Contact the following licensing organizations for your state to find out what the licensing requirements are for real estate agents, brokers, and appraisers. They may also be able to provide information on approved real estate training providers in the state.

Sales and Broker Licenses

The following real estate commissions or license law officials have information about the sales and broker license requirements in each state.

Alabama Real Estate Commission
1201 Carmichael Way
Montgomery, AL 36106
334-242-5544

Alaska Division of Occupational Licensing
Real Estate Commission
3601 C Street, Suite 722
Anchorage, AK 99503
907-269-8160

Arizona Department of Real Estate
2910 North 44th Street, Suite 100
Phoenix, AZ 85018
602-468-1414

Arkansas Real Estate Commission
612 South Summit Street
Little Rock, AR 72201-4740
501-682-2732

California Department of Real Estate
2201 Broadway
Sacramento, CA 95814
916-227-0782

Colorado Real Estate Commission
Department of Regulatory Agencies
1900 Grant Street, Suite 600
Denver, CO 80203
303-894-2166

Connecticut Department of Consumer Protection
Real Estate and Professional Trades Division
165 Capitol Avenue, Room 110
Hartford, CT 06106
860-566-3290

Delaware Real Estate Commission
861 Silver Lake Blvd., Suite 203
P.O. Box 1401
Dover, DE 19903
302-739-4522, ext. 219

District of Columbia Department of
Consumer and Regulatory Affairs
614 H Street N. W., Room 921
P. O. Box 37200
Washington, DC 20013-7200
202-727-7000

Florida Division of Real Estate
400 W. Robinson Street
P. O. Box 1900
Orlando, FL 32802-1900
407-425-0800

Georgia Real Estate Commission
International Tower, Suite 1000
229 Peachtree Street, N. W.
Atlanta, GA 30303-1605
404-656-3916

Hawaii Real Estate Commission
250 S. King Street, Room 702
Honolulu, HI 96813
808-586-2643

Idaho Real Estate Commission
P. O. Box 83720
Boise, ID 83720-0077
208-334-3285

Illinois Office of Banks and Real Estate
500 East Monroe Street, Suite 200
Springfield, IL 62701
217-785-9300

Indiana Professional Licensing Agency
302 W. Washington Street, EO34
Indianapolis, IN 46204
317-232-2980

Iowa Real Estate Commission
1918 S. E. Hulsizer Avenue
Ankeny, IA 50021-3941
515-281-3183

Kansas Real Estate Commission
3 Townsite Plaza, Suite 200
120 S.E. 6th Avenue
Topeka, KS 66603-3511
785-296-3411

Kentucky Real Estate Commission
10200 Linn Station Road, Suite 201
Louisville, KY 40223
502-425-4273

Louisiana Real Estate Commission
9071 Interline
P. O. Box 14785
Baton Rouge, LA 70898-1485
504-925-4788 or 800-821-4529

Maine Real Estate Commission
35 State House Station
Augusta, ME 04333-0035
207-624-8503

Maryland Real Estate Commission
501 St. Paul Place, 8th Floor
Baltimore, MD 21202-2272
410-333-8124

Massachusetts Real Estate Board
100 Cambridge Street, Room 1313
Boston, MA 02202
617-727-2373

Michigan Consumer and Industry Services
Office of Commercial Services
P. O. Box 30243
Lansing, MI 48909
517-241-9288

Minnesota Commerce Department
133 East 7th Street
St. Paul, MN 55101
612-296-4026

Mississippi Real Estate Commission
P. O. Box 12685
Jackson, MS 39236-2685
601-987-3969

Missouri Real Estate Commission
P. O. Box 1339
Jefferson City, MO 65102
573-751-2628

Montana Department of Commerce
Board of Realty Regulation
111 N. Jackson
P. O. Box 200513
Helena, MT 59620-0513
406-444-2961

Nebraska Real Estate Commission
1200 N Street, Suite 402
Lincoln, NE 68508
402-471-2004

Nevada Department of Business & Industry
Real Estate Division
2501 E. Sahara Avenue
Las Vegas, NE 89158
702-486-4033

New Hampshire Real Estate Commission
State House Annex, Room 437
25 Capitol Street
Concord, NH 03301-6312
603-271-2701

New Jersey Real Estate Commission
20 West State Street
P. O. Box 328
Trenton, NJ 08625-0328
609-292-8280

New Mexico Real Estate Commission
1650 University Blvd., N. E., Suite 490
Albuquerque, NM 87102
505-841-9120

New York Department of State
Division of Licensing
84 Holland Avenue
Albany, NY 12208
518-473-2728

North Carolina Real Estate Commission
P. O. Box 17100
Raleigh, NC 27619-7100
919-875-3700

North Dakota Real Estate Commission
314 East Thayer Avenue
P. O. Box 727
Bismarck, ND 58502-0727
701-328-9749

Ohio Division of Real Estate
77 South High Street, 20th Floor
Columbus, OH 43266-0547
614-466-4100

Oklahoma Real Estate Commission
4040 N. Lincoln Blvd., Suite 100
Oklahoma City, OK 73105
405-521-3387

Oregon Real Estate Agency
1177 Center Street, N.E.
Salem, OR 97310-2503
503-378-4170

Pennsylvania Real Estate Commission
P. O. Box 2649
Harrisburg, PA 17105-2649
717-783-3658

Rhode Island Department of Business Regulation
Licensing and Consumer Protection
233 Richmond Street
Providence, RI 02903
401-277-2255

South Carolina Real Estate Commission
P. O. Box 11847
Columbia, SC 29211-1847
803-896-4400

South Dakota Real Estate Commission
118 W. Capitol
Pierre, SD 57501
605-773-3600

Tennessee Real Estate Commission
500 James Robertson Pkwy, Suite 180
Davy Crockett Tower
Nashville, TN 37243-1151
615-741-2273

Texas Real Estate Commission
P. O. Box 12188
Austin, TX 78711-2188
512-459-6544

Utah Division of Real Estate
P. O. Box 146711
Salt Lake City, UT 84114-6711
801-530-6747

Vermont Real Estate Commission
109 State Street
Montpelier, VT 05609-1106
802-828-3228

Virginia Department of Professional
and Occupational Regulation
3600 West Broad Street
Richmond, VA 23230
804-367-8526

Washington Real Estate Program
Department of Licensing
P. O. Box 9015
Olympia, WA 98504-9015
360-586-6101

West Virginia Real Estate Commission
1033 Quarrier Street, Suite 400
Charleston, WV 25301-2315
304-558-3555

Wisconsin Real Estate Bureau
P. O. Box 8935
Madison, WI 53708
608-267-7134

Wyoming Real Estate Commission
2020 Carey Avenue, Suite 100
Cheyenne, WY 82002
307-777-7141

Appraiser Certification and Licensing

The following real estate commissions or appraisal boards have information about
the appraiser certification and licensing requirements in each state.

Alabama Real Estate Appraisal Board
660 Adams Avenue, Suite 360
Montgomery, AL 36104
205-242-8747

Alaska Department of Appraisal Certification
Juneau, AK 99101
907-465-2542

Arizona State Board of Appraisers
1700 W. Washington, Suite 133
Phoenix, AZ 85017
612-542-1539

Arkansas Appraiser Licensing and Certification Board
2725 Cantrell Road, Suite 202
Little Rock, AR 72202
501-324-9815

California Office of Real Estate Appraisers
1225 R Street
Sacramento, CA 95814-5812
916-322-2500

Colorado Board of Real Estate Appraisers
1900 Grant Street, Suite 600
Denver, CO 80203
303-894-2166

Connecticut Appraisal Board
165 Capitol Avenue
Hartford, CT 06106
203-566-5130

Delaware Council on Real Estate Appraisers
Margaret O'Neill Building
P. O. Box 1401
Dover, DE 19903
302-739-4522

District of Columbia Appraisal Board
614 H Street N. W.
Washington, DC 20013
202-727-7662

Florida Division of Real Estate Appraisers
400 W. Robinson Avenue
Orlando, FL 32801
407-423-6092

Georgia Appraiser's Board
148 International Boulevard, Suite 500
Atlanta, GA 30303-1734
404-656-3916

Hawaii Professional Licensure (Appraisal)
Department of Commerce and Consumer Affairs
P. O. Box 3469
Honolulu, HI 96813
808-586-2694

Idaho Bureau of Occupational Licenses
Real Estate Appraisal
Owyhee Plaza
109 Main Street, Suite 220
Boise, ID 83702
208-334-3233

Illinois Department of Professional Regulation
320 West Washington, Third Floor
Springfield, IL 62786
217-782-8556

Indiana Professional Licensing Agency
302 West Washington
Indianapolis, IN 46204-2700
317-232-2980

Iowa Professional Licensing and Regulation Division
Department of Commerce
Appraiser Certification
1918 S. E. Hulsizer Avenue
Ankeny, IA 50021
515-281-5602

Kansas Appraisal Board
3 Townsite Plaza, Suite 200
120 S. E. Sixth Avenue
Topeka, KS 66603-3511
913-296-0706

Kentucky Appraisal Board
3572 Iron Works Pike, Suite 308
Lexington, KY 45011-8410
606-255-0144

Louisiana Appraisal Board
P. O. Box 41046
Baton Rouge, LA 70809
504-923-0232

Maine State Board of Real Estate Appraisers
State House Station #35
Augusta, ME 04333
207-582-8723

Maryland Real Estate Commission Appraisal Board
501 St. Paul Place, 9th Floor
Baltimore, MD 21202
410-333-4517

Massachusetts Board of Registration of Real Estate Appraisers
100 Cambridge Street, Room 1512
Boston, MA 02202
617-727-3055

Michigan Department of Commerce
Board of Real Estate Appraisers
Lansing, MI 48909
517-373-0580

Minnesota Commerce Department
Real Estate Appraisal Division
133 E. Seventh Street
St. Paul, MN 55101
612-296-4328

Mississippi Real Estate Appraiser Licensing and Certification Board
1920 Dunbarton Drive
Jackson, MS 39216-5087
601-987-4150

Missouri Real Estate Appraisal Commission
P. O. Box 202
Jefferson City, MO 65102
314-751-0038

Montana Board of Appraisers
111 North Jackson
P. O. Box 200513
Helena, MT 59620-0513
406-444-3561

Nebraska Real Estate Appraisal Board
P. O. Box 94963
Lincoln, NE 68509-4963
402-471-9015

Nevada Real Estate Division
2501 East Sahara Avenue
Las Vegas, NV 89158
702-486-4033

New Hampshire Real Estate Appraiser Board
Waverly Square
6 Chenell Drive, Suite 290
Concord, NH 03301-8514
603-271-6186

New Jersey State Board of Real Estate Appraisers
P. O. Box 45032
Newark, NJ 07101
201-564-6480

New Mexico Appraisal Board
1599 St. Francis Drive
P. O. Box 25101
Santa Fe, NM 87505
505-827-7554

New York Department of State
Division of Licensing Services
84 Holland Avenue
Albany, NY 12208
518-474-4429

North Carolina Appraisal Board
P. O. Box 33189
Charlotte, NC 28242
704-383-6624

North Dakota Real Estate Appraisal Board
P. O. Box 1336
Bismarck, ND 58502-1336
701-222-1051

Ohio Division of Real Estate
Appraisal Section
615 West Superior Avenue, Room 525
Cleveland, OH 44113
216-787-3100

Oklahoma Real Estate Appraisal Board
Department of Insurance
P. O. Box 53408
Oklahoma City, OK 73152
405-521-6636

Oregon Appraisal Certification and Licensure Board
21 Labor and Industries Building
Salem, OR 97310
503-373-1505

Pennsylvania State Board of Real Estate Appraisers
P. O. Box 2649
Harrisburg, PA 17105-2649
717-783-4866

Rhode Island Department of Business Regulation
Licensing and Consumer Protection
233 Richmond Street
Providence, RI 02903
401-277-2262

South Carolina Real Estate Appraisers Board
1201 Main Street, Suite 1530
Columbia, SC 29201
803-737-0898

South Dakota Real Estate Appraisal Regulatory Commission
910 East Sioux Avenue
Pierre, SD 57501-0490
605-773-4608

Tennessee Real Estate Appraiser Commission
500 James Robertson Parkway, Suite 180
Nashville, TN 37243-1166
615-741-1831

Texas Appraiser Licensing and Certification Board
P. O. Box 12188
Austin, TX 78711-2188
512-465-3950

Utah Department of Commerce
Division of Real Estate
P. O. Box 45802
160 East 300 South
Salt Lake City, UT 84145-0806
801-530-6747

Vermont Board of Real Estate Appraisers
109 State Street
Montpelier, VT 05609-1106
802-828-2191

Virginia Department of Professional and Occupational Regulation
3600 West Broad Street
Richmond, VA 23230-4196
804-367-0500

Washington Real Estate Appraiser Section
Department of Licensing Services
P. O. Box 9012
Olympia, WA 98507-9012
206-753-1062

West Virginia Real Estate Appraiser Licensing and Certification Board
814 Virginia Street East, Suite 212
Charleston, WV 24301-2826
304-558-3919

Wisconsin Real Estate Appraisal Board
Department of Regulation and Licensing
1400 East Washington
P. O. Box 8935
Madison, WI 53708-8935
608-266-3423

Wyoming Real Estate Commission
Appraiser Licensure
205 Barrett Building
Cheyenne, WY 82002
307-777-7141

National Accrediting Agencies

Here is a list of national accrediting agencies for you to contact to see if your chosen school is accredited. You can request a list of schools that each agency accredits.

Accrediting Commission for Career Schools
and Colleges of Technology
Thomas A. Kube, Executive Director
2101 Wilson Boulevard, Suite 302
Arlington, VA 22201
703-247-4212
FAX: 703-247-4533

Accrediting Council for Independent
Colleges and Schools
Stephen D. Parker, Executive Director
750 First Street, NE, Suite 980
Washington, DC 20002-4241
202-336-6780
FAX: 202-842-2593

Distance Education and Training Council
Michael P. Lambert, Executive Secretary
1601 Eighteenth Street, NW
Washington, DC 20009-2529
202-234-5100
FAX: 202-332-1386

Regional Accrediting Agencies

If your school is not accredited by one of the national agencies, it may be accredited by a regional accrediting agency. Here is a list of regional agencies that you can contact to see if your chosen school is accredited. They are organized by broad geographic regions.

Middle States

Middle States Association of Colleges and Schools
Commission on Institutions of Higher Education
3624 Market Street
Philadelphia, PA 19104-2680
215-662-5606
FAX: 215-662-5950

New England States

Charles M. Cook, Director
New England Association of Schools and Colleges
Commission on Institutions of Higher Education
209 Burlington Road
Bedford, MA 07130-1433
617-271-0022
FAX: 617-271-0950

Richard E. Mandeville, Director
New England Association of Schools and Colleges
Commission on Vocational, Technical and Career Institution
209 Burlington Road
Bedford, MA 01730-1433
617-271-0022
FAX: 617-271-0950

North Central States

Steve Crow, Executive Director
North Central Association of Colleges and Schools
Commission on Institutions of Higher Education
30 North LaSalle, Suite 2400
Chicago, IL 60602-2504
312-263-0456
FAX: 312-263-7462

Northwest States

Sandra Elman, Executive Director
Northwest Association of Schools and Colleges
Commission on Colleges
11130 NE 33rd Place, Suite 120
Bellevue, WA 98004
206-827-2005
FAX: 206-827-3395

Southern States

James T. Rogers, Executive Director
Southern Association of Colleges and Schools
Commission on Colleges
1866 Southern Lane
Decatur, GA 30033-4097
404-679-4500 / 800-248-7701
FAX: 404-679-4558

Western States

David B. Wolf, Executive Director
Western Association of Schools and Colleges
Accrediting Commission for Community and Junior Colleges
3402 Mendocino Ave.
Santa Rosa, CA 95403-2244
707-569-9177
FAX: 707-569-9179

Ralph A. Wolff, Executive Director
Western Association of Schools and Colleges
Accrediting Commission for Senior Colleges and Universities
c/o Mills College, Box 9990
Oakland, CA 94613-0990
510-632-5000
FAX: 510-632-8361

State Higher Education or Financial Assistance Agencies

You can request information about financial aid from each of the following state higher education agencies and governing boards. Internet addresses have been included when available.

Alabama Commission on Higher Education
3465 Norman Bridge Road, Suite 205
Montgomery, AL 36105-2310
334-281-1998

Alaska Commission on Postsecondary Education
3030 Vintage Boulevard
Juneau, AK 99801-7109
907-465-2962
http://sygov.swadm.alaska.edu/BOR/

Arizona Commission for Postsecondary Education
2020 North Central Ave., Suite 275
Phoenix, AZ 85004-4503
602-229-2531
http://www.abor.asu.edu/

Arkansas Department of Higher Education
114 East Capitol Street
Little Rock, AK 72201-3818
501-324-9300

California Student Aid Commission
P. O. Box 510845
Sacramento, CA 94245-0845
916-445-0880
http://www.ucop.edu/ucophome/system/regents.html

Colorado Commission on Higher Education
Colorado Heritage Center
1300 Broadway, 2nd Floor
Denver, CO 80203
303-866-2723
http://www.state.co.us/edu_dir/state_hredu_dept.html

Connecticut Department of Higher Education
61 Woodland Street
Hartford, CT 06105-2391
203-566-3910
http://www.lib.uconn.edu/ConnState/HigherEd/dhe.htm

Delaware Higher Education Commission
Carvel State Office Building, Fourth Floor
820 North French Street
Wilmington, DE 19801
302-577-3240
http://www.state.de.us/high-ed/commiss/webpage.htm

District of Columbia Department of Human Services
Office of Postsecondary Education, Research and Assistance
2100 Martin Luther King, Jr., Avenue, S. E., Suite 401
Washington, DC 20020
202-727-3685

Florida Department of Education
Office of Student Financial Assistance
1344 Florida Education Center
325 West Gaines Street
Tallahassee, FL 32399-0400
904-487-0649
http://www.nwrdc.fsu.edu/bor/

Georgia Student Finance Authority
State Loans and Grants Division
2082 East Exchange Place, Suite 245
Tucker, GA 30084
404-414-3000
http://www.peachnet.edu/BORWEB/

Hawaii State Postsecondary Education Commission
2444 Dole Street, Room 202
Honolulu, HI 96822-2394
808-956-8213
http://www.hern.hawaii.edu/hern/

Idaho State Department of Education
650 West State Street
Boise, ID 83720
208-334-2113
http://www.sde.state.id.us/

Illinois Student Assistance Commission
1755 Lake Cook Road
Deerfield, IL 60015-5209
708-948-8500

State Student Assistance Commission of Indiana
150 West Market Street, Suite 500
Indianapolis, IN 46204-2811
317-232-2350
http://www.ai.org/ssaci/

Iowa College Student Aid Commission
914 Grand Avenue, Suite 201
Des Moines, IA 50309-2824
800-383-4222
http://www.state.ia.us/government/icsac/index.htm

Kansas Board of Regents
700 S. W. Harrison, Suite 1410
Topeka, KS 66603-3760
913-296-3517

Kentucky Higher Education Assistance Authority
1050 U. S. 127 South, Suite 102
Frankfort, KY 40601-4323
800-928-8926

Louisiana Student Financial Assistance Commission
Office of Student Financial Assistance
P. O. Box 91202
Baton Rouge, LA 70821-9202
800-259-5626

Finance Authority of Maine
P. O. Box 949
Augusta, ME 04333-0949
207-287-3263
http://www.maine.edu

Maryland Higher Education Commission
16 Francis Street, Jeffrey Building
Annapolis, MD 21401-1781
410-974-2971
http://www.ubalt.edu/www/mhec/

Massachusetts Board of Higher Education
330 Stuart Street
Boston, MA 02116
617-727-9420

Michigan Higher Education Assistance Authority
Office of Scholarships and Grants
P. O. Box 30462
Lansing, MI 48909-7962
517-373-3394

Minnesota Higher Education Services Office
Capitol Square Bldg., Suite 400
550 Cedar Street
St. Paul, MN 55101-2292
800-657-3866
gopher://gopher.hecb.state.mn.us/

Mississippi Postsecondary Education
Financial Assistance Board
3825 Ridgewood Road
Jackson, MS 39211-6453
601-982-6663

Missouri Coordinating Board for Higher Education
3515 Amazonas Drive
Jefferson City, MO 65109-5717
314-751-2361
gopher://dp.mocbhe.gov/

Montana University System
2500 Broadway
Helena, MT 59620-3103
406-444-6570
http://www.montana.edu/~aircj/manual/bor/

Nebraska Coordinating Commission
  for Postsecondary Education
P. O. Box 95005
Lincoln, NE 68509-5005
402-471-2847

Nevada Department of Education
400 West King Street
Capitol Complex
Carson City, NV 89710
702-687-5915
http://nsn.scs.unr.edu/nvdoe/

New Hampshire Postsecondary Education Commission
2 Industrial Park Drive
Concord, NH 03301-8512
603-271-2555

State of New Jersey
Office of Student Financial Assistance
4 Quakerbridge Plaza, CN 540
Trenton, NJ 08625
800-792-8670
http://ww.state.nj.us/highereducation/

New Mexico Commission on Higher Education
1068 Cerrillos Road
Santa Fe, NM 87501-4925
505-827-7383
http://www.nmche.org/index.html

New York State Higher Education Services Corporation
One Commerce Plaza
Albany, NY 12255
518-474-5642
http://hesc.state.ny.us

North Carolina State Education Assistance Authority
P. O. Box 2688
Chapel Hill, NC 27515-2688
919-821-4771

North Dakota University System
North Dakota Student Financial Assistance Program
600 East Boulevard Avenue
Bismarck, ND 58505-0230
701-224-4114

Ohio Student Aid Commission
P. O. Box 182452
309 South Fourth Street
Columbus, OH 43218-2452
800-837-6752
http://www.bor.ohio.gov

Oklahoma Guaranteed Student Loan Program
P. O. Box 3000
Oklahoma City, OK 73101-3000
405-858-4300 / 800-247-0420
http://www.ogslp.org

Oregon State System of Higher Education
700 Pringle Parkway, S. E.
Salem, OR 97310-0290
503-378-5585
http://www.osshe.edu/

Pennsylvania Higher Education Assistance Agency
1200 North Seventh Street
Harrisburg, PA 17102-1444
800-692-7435
http://sshe2.sshechan.edu/sshe.html

Rhode Island Higher Education Assistance Authority
560 Jefferson Boulevard
Warwick, RI 02886
800-922-9855

South Carolina Higher Education Tuition Grants Commission
1310 Lady Street, Suite 811
P. O. Box 12159
Columbia, SC 29201
803-734-1200
http://che400.state.sc.us

South Dakota Department of Education and Cultural Affairs
Office of the Secretary
700 Governors Drive
Pierre, SD 57501-2291
605-773-3134
http://www.state.sd.us/state/executive/deca/deca.html

Tennessee Higher Education Commission
404 James Robertson Parkway, Suite 1900
Nashville, TN 37243-0820
615-741-3605
http://www.TBR.state.tn.us

Texas Higher Education Coordinating Board
P. O. Box 12788, Capitol Station
Austin, TX 78711
800-242-3062
http://www.texas.gov/agency/781.html

Utah State Board of Regents
Utah System of Higher Education
355 West North Temple
#3 Triad Center, Suite 550
Salt Lake City, UT 84180-1205
801-321-7205
http://www.gv.ex.state.ut.us/highered.htm

Vermont Student Assistance Corporation
Champlain Mill
P. O. Box 2000
Winooski, VT 05404-2601
800-642-3177
http://www.vsac.org

Virginia Council of Higher Education
James Monroe Building
101 North Fourteenth Street
Richmond, VA 23219
804-786-1690
http://www.schev.edu

Washington Higher Education Coordinating Board
P. O. Box 43430
917 Lakeridge Way, S. W.
Olympia, WA 98504-3430
206-753-7850

State College & University Systems Central Office
1018 Kanawha Boulevard East, Suite 700
Charleston, WV 25301-2827
304-558-4016
http://www.scusco.wvnet.edu/

Wisconsin Higher Educational Aid Board
P. O. Box 7885
Madison, WI 53707-7885
608-267-2206
http://www.uwsa.edu/

Wyoming Student Financial Aid
University Station, Box 3335
Laramie, WY 82071
307-777-7763

U.S. DEPARTMENT OF EDUCATION
Office of Postsecondary Education
Student Financial Assistance Programs
Pell and State Grant Section
U. S. Department of Education
ROB #3, Room 3045
600 Independence Avenue, S. W.
Washington, DC 20202-5447
202-708-4607

Division of Higher Education Incentive Programs
Higher Education Programs
Office of Postsecondary Education
U. S. Department of Education
1280 Maryland Avenue, S. W., Suite C80
Washington, DC 20024

APPENDIX B

For more information on the topics discussed in this book, refer to the following reading list organized by subject. This list of helpful books is followed by a list of periodicals related to the real estate profession.

ADDITIONAL RESOURCES

BOOKS

Career Information

Cosgrove, Holli R. *Encyclopedia of Careers and Vocational Guidance, 10th Edition.* J.G. Ferguson Pub. 1997.

U. S. Department of Labor. *Occupational Outlook Handbook.* VGM Career Horizons. 1996.

College Guides

The College Board. *The College Handbook 1998, 35th Edition.* College Entrance Exam Board. 1997.

Peterson's Vocational and Technical Schools: East, 3rd Edition. Peterson's Guides. 1998.

Peterson's Vocational and Technical Schools: West, 3rd Edition. Peterson's Guides. 1998.

The Princeton Review. *The Complete Book of Colleges 1998.* Random House, The Princeton Review. 1997.

Cover Letters

Beatty, Richard H. *The Perfect Cover Letter, 2nd Edition.* John Wiley & Sons. 1997.

Marler, Patty and Jan Bailey Mattia. *Cover Letters Made Easy.* NTC Pub. 1996.

Wood, John. *How to Write Attention-Grabbing Query & Cover Letters.* Writers Digest Books. 1996.

Distance Education

Duffy, James P. *College Online: How to Take College Courses Without Leaving Home.* John Wiley & Sons. 1997

Miller, Inabeth et al. *Kaplan Distance Learning.* Simon & Schuster. 1997

Thorson, Marcie Kisner. *Campus-Free College Degrees, 8th Edition.* Thorson Guides. 1998

Financial Aid

College School Service. *College Costs & Financial Aid Handbook, 18th Edition.* The College Entrance Examination Board. 1998.

Davis, Kristen. *Financing College: How To Use Savings, Financial Aid, Scholarships, and Loans to Afford the School of Your Choice.* Random House. 1996.

Schwartz, John. *College Scholarships and Financial Aid, 7th Edition.* ARCO. 1997.

Interviews

Bloch, Deborah P., Ph.D. *How to Have a Winning Interview.* VGM Career Horizons. 1996.

Fry, Ron. *101 Great Answers to the Toughest Interview Questions, 3rd Edition.* Book-Mart Press. 1996.

Kennedy, Joyce Lain. *Job Interviews for Dummies.* IDG Books. 1996.

Krannich, Caryl Rae, and Ronald L. Krannich. *101 Dynamite Answers to Interview Questions : Sell Your Strengths, 3rd Edition.* Impact Publications. 1997.

Job Hunting

Adams Media Corporation, Editor. *Adams Jobs Almanac 1998.* Adams Publishers. 1997.

Bolles, Richard Nelson. *What Color is your Parachute?* Ten Speed Press. 1997.

Cubbage, Sue A. and Marcia P. Williams. *The 1996 National Job Hotline Directory.* McGraw-Hill. 1996

Sonnenblick, Carol, Michaele Basciano, and Kim Crabbe. *Job Hunting Made Easy: 20 Simple Steps to Coming Up a Winner.* LearningExpress. 1997.

Networking

Fisher, Donna and Sandy Vilas. *Power Networking: 55 Secrets for Personal and Professional Success.* MountainHarbour Publications. 1994.

National Business Employment Weekly. *Networking: Insider's Strategies for Tapping the Hidden Market Where Most Jobs are Found.* John Wiley & Sons. 1994.

Shelly, Susan. *Networking for Novices: The Basics Made Easy.* LearningExpress. 1998.

Real Estate Appraisal

Betts, Richard M. and Silas Ely. *Basic Real Estate Appraisal, 3rd Edition*. Prentice-Hall. 1994.

Boykin, James H. and Alfred A. Ring. *The Valuation of Real Estate. 4th Edition*. Prentice-Hall. 1993.

Ventolo, William, Martha Williams, Dennis Tosh, and William Rayburn, Eds. *Fundamentals of Real Estate Appraisal, 7th Edition*. Real Estate Education Company. 1998.

Real Estate Law, Finance, and Math

Armbrust, Betty J., Hugh H. Bradley, and John W. Armbrust. *Practical Real Estate Math*. Gorsuch Scarisbrick Publishers. 1991.

Karp, James, Elliot Klayman, and Frank Gibson. *Real Estate Law, 4th Edition*. Real Estate Education Company. 1998.

Sirota, David. *Essentials of Real Estate Finance, 9th Edition*. Real Estate Education Company. 1997.

Ventolo, William L., Jr., Ralph Tamper, and Wellington Allaway. *Mastering Real Estate Math, 6th Edition*, Real Estate Education Company. 1995.

Werner, Raymond J. and Robert Kratovil. *Real Estate Law, 10th Edition*. Prentice-Hall. 1993.

Real Estate Property Management

Kyle, Robert and Floyd Baird. *Property Management, 5th Edition*. Real Estate Education Company. 1995.

Reed, John T. *How to Manage Residential Property for Maximum Cash Flow and Resale Value, 2nd Edition*. Reed Publishing. 1995.

Real Estate Sales and Management

Cortesi, Gerald. *Mastering Real Estate Principles.* Real Estate Education Company. 1996.

Cross, Carla. *Up and Running in 30 Days: Make Money Your First Month in Real Estate.* Real Estate Education Company. 1995.

Gaddy, Wade E., Jr. and Robert E. Hart. *Real Estate Fundamentals, 4th Edition.* Real Estate Education Company. 1995.

Galaty, Fillmore W., Wellington J. Allaway, and Robert C. Kyle. *Modern Real Estate Practice, 14th Edition.* Real Estate Education Co. 1997.

Geschwender, Arlyne. *Real Estate Principles and Practices, 4th Edition.* Gorsuch Scarisbrick Publishers. 1994.

Jacobus, Charles, and Bruce Harwood. *Real Estate: An Introduction to the Profession, 7th Edition.* Prentice Hall. 1996.

Kersnar, Scott. *Net Success: How Real Estate Agents Use the Internet.* Co-published by Songline Studios and O'Reilly & Associates, Inc. 1996.

Lindeman, Bruce. *Real Estate Brokerage Management, 3rd Edition.* Prentice-Hall. 1993.

Lyons, Gail, and Don Harlan. *Buyer Agency: Your Competitive Edge in Real Estate, 3rd Edition.* Real Estate Education Company. 1997.

Lyons, Gail, Donald Harlan, and John Tuccillo. *The Future of Real Estate: Profiting from the Revolution.* Real Estate Education Company. 1996.

Real Estate Brokerage Council. *Real Estate Office Management, 3rd Edition.* Real Estate Education Company. 1996.

Resumes

Adams Resume Almanac & Disc. Adams Media Corporation. 1996.

Haft, Timothy D. *Trashproof Resumes: Your Guide to Cracking the Job Market.* Princeton Review. 1995.

Resumes! Resumes! Resumes!: Top Career Experts Show You the Job-Landing Resumes that Sold Them, 3rd Edition. Book-Mart Press-Career Press. 1997.

Scholarship Guides

Peterson's Scholarships, Grants & Prizes 1998 : The Most Complete Guide to College Financial Aid from Private Sources. Peterson's Guides. 1997.

Ragins, Marianne. *Winning Scholarships for College: An Insider's Guide.* Henry Holt & Co. 1994.

Scholarships 1998. Simon & Schuster, Kaplan. 1997.

Vuturo, Christopher. *The Scholarship Advisor: More Than 500,000 Scholarships Worth 1.5 Billion Dollars 1998.* Princeton Review. 1997.

Study Skills Improvement

Chesla, Elizabeth. *Read Better, Remember More: The Basics Made Easy.* Learning-Express. 1997.

Coman, Marcia J. and Kathy L. Heavers. *How to Improve Your Study Skills, 2nd Edition.* NTC Publishing Group. 1998.

Olson, Judith F. *Grammar Essentials: The Basics Made Easy.* LearningExpress. 1997.

Robinovitz, Judith. *Practical Math Success in 20 Minutes a Day.* LearningExpress. 1997.

Wood, Gail. *How to Study: The Basics Made Easy.* LearningExpress. 1997.

Test Preparation

AMP Real Estate Sales Exam. LearningExpress. 1998.

ASI Real Estate Sales Exam. LearningExpress. 1998.

Fisher, Jeffrey D., and Dennis S. Tosh. *Questions & Answers to Help You Pass the Real Estate Appraisal Exams,* 2nd Edition. Real Estate Education Company. 1994.

Katyman, John and Adam Robinson. *Cracking the SAT & PSAT, 1998 Edition.* Random House, The Princeton Review. 1997.

Martz, Geoff, Kim Magloire, and Theodore Silver. *Cracking the ACT, 97–98 Edition.* Random House, The Princeton Review. 1997.

Meyers, Judith N. *Secrets of Taking Any Test: The Basics Made Easy.* LearningExpress. 1997.

PSI Real Estate Sales Exam. LearningExpress. 1998.

Texas Real Estate Sales Exam. LearningExpress. 1998.

Work Relationships

Bell, Arthur H., and Dayle M. Smith. *Winning With Difficult People, 2nd Edition.* Barron's Educational Series. 1997.

Bramson, Robert M., Ph.D. *Coping With Difficult Bosses.* Simon and Schuster. 1994.

Felder, Leonard, *Does Someone at Work Treat You Badly?* Berkley Books. 1993.

To order any LearningExpress publication, call toll-free:
1-888-551-5627.

Periodicals Related to Real Estate

Here are some magazines and journals that might interest you.

The Appraisal Journal
Published by the Appraisal Institute
875 N. Michigan Avenue, Suite 2400
Attn: Subscription Department
Chicago, IL 60611-1980
312-335-4427
FAX: 312-335-4200

Commercial Investment Real Estate Journal
Publication of the Commercial Investment Real Estate Institute
430 N. Michigan Avenue
Chicago, IL 60611
312-321-4460

The Communicator
Publication of the Foundation of Real Estate Appraisers
4907 Morena Blvd., Suite 1415
San Diego, CA 92117
800-882-4410
FAX: 619-483-2490

Journal of Property Management
Institute of Real Estate Management
430 N. Michigan Avenue
Chicago, IL 60610
312-661-1930

Journal of Real Estate Portfolio Management and
Journal of Real Estate Research
American Real Estate Society
Theron R. Nelson
College of Business and Public Administration
University of North Dakota

Grand Forks, ND 58202-71202
701-777-3670
htttp://www.ARESnet.org

National Real Estate Investor
6151 Powers Ferry Road
Atlanta, GA 30339
404-955-2500

The Real Estate Professional
Wellesley Publications
1492 Highland Avenue
Needham, MA 02192
617-729-0935

Today's REALTOR® Magazine
A publication of the National Association of Realtors®
700 11th St. NW
Washington, DC 20001-4507
FAX: 202/383-1231
E-mail: narpubs@realtors.org